PEARSON
Literature

Student Companion All-in-One Workbook

GRADE 9

PEARSON

NEW YORK, NEW YORK • BOSTON, MASSACHUSETTS
CHANDLER, ARIZONA • GLENVIEW, ILLINOIS

Copyright © by Pearson Education, Inc., or its affiliates. All Rights Reserved. Printed in the United States of America. This publication is protected by copyright, and permission should be obtained from the publisher prior to any prohibited reproduction, storage in a retrieval system, or transmission in any form or by any means, electronic, mechanical, photocopying, recording, or otherwise. For information regarding permissions, request forms, and the appropriate contacts within the Pearson Education Global Rights & Permissions department, please visit www.pearsoned.com/permissions.

PEARSON and ALWAYS LEARNING are exclusive trademarks owned by Pearson Education, Inc. or its affiliates, in the U.S. and/or other countries.

Unless otherwise indicated herein, any third-party trademarks that may appear in this work are the property of their respective owners and any references to third-party trademarks, logos, or other trade dress are for demonstrative or descriptive purposes only. Such references are not intended to imply any sponsorship, endorsement, authorization, or promotion of Pearson's products by the owners of such marks, or any relationship between the owner and Pearson Education, Inc. or its affiliates, authors, licensees, or distributors.

PEARSON

ISBN-13: 978-0-13-327118-8
ISBN-10: 0-13-327118-8

CONTENTS

UNIT 1 • PART 1 Setting Expectations
Big Question Vocabulary 1 1
Big Question Vocabulary 2 2
Big Question Vocabulary 3 3
Applying the Big Question 4

UNIT 1 • PART 2 Guided Exploration
"The Most Dangerous Game" by Richard Connell
Writing About the Big Question 5
Literary Analysis: Conflict 6
Reading: Use Details to Make Inferences 7
Vocabulary Builder 8
Conventions: Parts of Speech 9
Support for Writing to Sources: Comparison-and-Contrast Essay 10
Support for Speaking and Listening: Oral Presentation 11

"The Gift of the Magi" by O. Henry
Writing About the Big Question 12
Literary Analysis: Irony and Surprise Ending 13
Reading: Use Prior Knowledge and Experience to Make Inferences 14
Vocabulary Builder 15
Conventions: Simple and Perfect Tenses 16
Support for Writing to Sources: Narrative Text (News Report) 17
Support for Speaking and Listening: Debate 18

"Rules of the Game" by Amy Tan
Writing About the Big Question 19
Literary Analysis: Character and Characterization 20
Reading: Ask Questions to Analyze Cause and Effect 21
Vocabulary Builder 22
Conventions: Subjects and Predicates 23
Support for Writing to Sources: Informative Text 24
Support for Research and Technology: Informative Brochure 25

"The Cask of Amontillado" by Edgar Allan Poe
Writing About the Big Question 26
Literary Analysis: Plot, Foreshadowing, and Suspense 27
Reading: Read Ahead to Make and Verify Predictions 28
Vocabulary Builder 29

All-in-One Workbook
© Pearson Education, Inc. All rights reserved.

    Conventions: Active Voice and Passive Voice 30
    Support for Writing to Sources: Argumentative Text 31
    Support for Speaking and Listening: Retelling 32

Comparing Texts: "Checkouts" by Cynthia Rylant and
"The Girl Who Can" by Ama Ata Aidoo
    Writing About the Big Question 33
    Literary Analysis: Point of View 34
    Vocabulary Builder 35
    Support for Writing to Sources: Explanatory Text 36

Writing Process 37
Writer's Toolbox: Conventions 38

UNIT 1 • PART 3 Developing Insights
"The Scarlet Ibis" by James Hurst
    Vocabulary Builder 39
    Take Notes for Discussion 40
    Take Notes for Writing to Sources 41
    Take Notes for Research 42

"Much Madness is divinest sense" by Emily Dickinson
    Vocabulary Builder 43

"My English" by Julia Alvarez
    Vocabulary Builder 44
    Take Notes for Discussion 45
    Take Notes for Research 46
    Take Notes for Writing to Sources 47

"The Case for Fitting In" by David Berreby
    Vocabulary Builder 48
    Take Notes for Discussion 49
    Take Notes for Research 50
    Take Notes for Writing to Sources 51

"The Geeks Shall Inherit the Earth" by Alexandra Robbins
    Vocabulary Builder 52
    Take Notes for Discussion 53
    Take Notes for Research 54
    Take Notes for Writing to Sources 55

from "Blue Nines and Red Words" by Daniel Tammet
  Vocabulary Builder 56
  Take Notes for Discussion 57
  Take Notes for Research 58
  Take Notes for Writing to Sources 59

New Yorker Cartoon
  Vocabulary Builder and Take Notes for Writing to Sources 60

UNIT 2 • PART 1 Setting Expectations
Big Question Vocabulary 1 61
Big Question Vocabulary 2 62
Big Question Vocabulary 3 63
Applying the Big Question 64

UNIT 2 • PART 2 Guided Exploration
"On Summer" by Lorraine Hansberry
  Writing About the Big Question 65
  Literary Analysis: Style 66
  Reading: Generate Prior Questions to Identify Main Idea and Details 67
  Vocabulary Builder 68
  Conventions: Direct and Indirect Objects 69
  Support for Writing to Sources: Response to Literature 70
  Support for Speaking and Listening: Panel Dicussion 71

"The News" by Neil Postman
  Writing About the Big Question 72
  Literary Analysis: Expository Essay 73
  Reading: Reread to Identify Main Idea and Details 74
  Vocabulary Builder 75
  Conventions: Predicate Nominatives and Predicate Adjectives 76
  Support for Writing to Sources: Explanatory Essay 77
  Support for Research and Technology: Journal Entries 78

"Libraries Face Sad Chapter" by Pete Hamill
  Writing About the Big Question 79
  Literary Analysis: Persuasive Essay 80
  Reading: Reread to Analyze and Evaluate Persuasive Appeals 81

    Vocabulary Builder... 82
    Conventions: Colons, Semicolons, and Ellipsis Points.......................... 83
    Support for Writing to Sources: Informative Text (Abstract)................... 84
    Support for Research and Technology: Build and Present Knowledge.............. 85

"I Have a Dream" by Martin Luther King, Jr.
    Writing About the Big Question.. 86
    Literary Analysis: Persuasive Speech... 87
    Reading: Evaluate Persuasion... 88
    Vocabulary Builder... 89
    Conventions: Independent and Dependent Clauses................................. 90
    Support for Writing to Sources: Proposal....................................... 91
    Support for Speaking and Listening: Radio News Report.......................... 92

Comparing Texts: *from* Silent Spring by Rachel Carson and "If I Forget Thee, Oh Earth ..." by Arthur C. Clarke
    Writing About the Big Question.. 93
    Literary Analysis: Theme... 94
    Vocabulary Builder... 95
    Support for Writing to Sources: Explanatory Text............................... 96

Writing Process... 97
Writing Toolbox: Conventions... 98

UNIT 2 • PART 3 Developing Insights
First Inaugural Address by Franklin Delano Roosevelt
    Vocabulary Builder... 99
    Take Notes for Discussion... 100
    Take Notes for Writing to Sources... 101
    Take Notes for Research... 102

***from* Nothing to Fear: Lessons in Leadership from FDR by Alan Axelrod**
    Vocabulary Builder.. 103
    Take Notes for Discussion... 104
    Take Notes for Research... 105
    Take Notes for Writing to Sources... 106

***from* Americans in the Great Depression by Eric Rauchway**
    Vocabulary Builder.. 107
    Take Notes for Discussion... 108
    Take Notes for Research... 109
    Take Notes for Writing to Sources... 110

from **Women on the Breadlines** by Meridel Le Sueur
   Vocabulary Builder 111
   Take Notes for Discussion 112
   Take Notes for Research 113
   Take Notes for Writing to Sources 114

"Bread Line, New York City, 1932" by H. W. Fechner
   Vocabulary Builder and Take Notes for Writing to Sources 115

UNIT 3 • PART 1 Setting Expectations
Big Question Vocabulary 1 116
Big Question Vocabulary 2 117
Big Question Vocabulary 3 118
Applying the Big Question 119

UNIT 3 • PART 2 Guided Exploration
Poetry Collection 1: Langston Hughes, Emily Dickinson, Gabriela Mistral, Jean de Sponde
   Writing About the Big Question 120
   Literary Analysis: Figurative Language 121
   Reading: Read Fluently 122
   Vocabulary Builder 123
   Conventions: Prepositions and Prepositional Phrases 124
   Support for Writing to Sources: Informative Text 125
   Support for Speaking and Listening: Speech 126

Poetry Collection 2: Yusef Komunyakaa, Lewis Carroll, Edgar Allan Poe, May Swenson
   Writing About the Big Question 127
   Literary Analysis: Sound Devices 128
   Reading: Read Fluently 129
   Vocabulary Builder 130
   Conventions: Participles and Participial Phrases, Gerunds and Gerund Phrases 131
   Support for Writing to Sources: Argument 132
   Support for Speaking and Listening: Presentation of Ideas 133

Poetry Collection 3: Ernest Lawrence Thayer, William Stafford, Sandra Cisneros, Edgar Allan Poe
   Writing About the Big Question 134
   Literary Analysis: Narrative Poetry 135

Reading: Paraphrasing 136
Vocabulary Builder 137
Conventions: Appositive and Absolute Phrases 138
Support for Writing to Sources: Informative Text 139
Support for Speaking and Listening: Dialogue 140

Poetry Collection 4: Robert Frost, Emily Dickinson, T. S. Eliot, William Shakespeare
Writing About the Big Question 141
Literary Analysis: Rhyme and Meter 142
Reading: Paraphrasing 143
Vocabulary Builder 144
Conventions: Infinitives and Infinitive Phrases 145
Support for Writing to Sources: Poem 146
Support for Speaking and Listening: Panel Discussion 147

Comparing Texts: Poetry by Alice Walker, Bashō, Chiyojo, Walt Whitman, William Shakespeare
Writing About the Big Question 148
Literary Analysis: Lyric Poetry 149
Vocabulary Builder 150
Support for Writing to Sources: Explanatory Text 151

Writing Process 152
Writer's Toolbox: Conventions 153

UNIT 3 • PART 3 Developing Insights

"The Assassination of John F. Kennedy" by Gwendolyn Brooks and "Instead of an Elegy" by G. S. Fraser
Vocabulary Builder 154
Take Notes for Discussion 155
Take Notes for Writing to Sources 156
Take Notes for Research 157

from **A White House Diary** by Lady Bird Johnson
Vocabulary Builder 158
Take Notes for Discussion 159
Take Notes for Research 160
Take Notes for Writing to Sources 161

"American History" by Judith Ortiz Cofer
   Vocabulary Builder..162
   Take Notes for Discussion..163
   Take Notes for Research...164
   Take Notes for Writing to Sources...165

Address Before a Joint Session of the Congress, November 27, 1963, by Lyndon Baines Johnson
   Vocabulary Builder..166
   Take Notes for Discussion..167
   Take Notes for Research...168
   Take Notes for Writing to Sources...169

Images of a Tragedy
   Vocabulary Builder and Take Notes for Writing to Sources................170

UNIT 4 • PART 1 Setting Expectations
Big Question Vocabulary 1..171
Big Question Vocabulary 2..172
Big Question Vocabulary 3..173
Applying the Big Question..174

UNIT 4 • PART 2 Guided Exploration
The Tragedy of Romeo and Juliet, *Act I*, by William Shakespeare
   Writing About the Big Question..175
   Literary Analysis: Dialogue and Stage Directions..........................176
   Reading: Summarize..177
   Vocabulary Builder..178

The Tragedy of Romeo and Juliet, *Act II*, by William Shakespeare
   Writing About the Big Question..179
   Literary Analysis: Blank Verse..180
   Reading: Read in Sentences..181
   Vocabulary Builder..182

The Tragedy of Romeo and Juliet, *Act III*, by William Shakespeare
   Writing About the Big Question..183
   Literary Analysis: Dramatic Speeches......................................184
   Reading: Paraphrase...185
   Vocabulary Builder..186

All-in-One Workbook
© Pearson Education, Inc. All rights reserved.

The Tragedy of Romeo and Juliet, *Act IV*, by William Shakespeare
    Writing About the Big Question 187
    Literary Analysis: Dramatic Irony 188
    Reading: Break Down Long Sentences 189
    Vocabulary Builder 190

The Tragedy of Romeo and Juliet, *Act V*, by William Shakespeare
    Writing About the Big Question 191
    Literary Analysis: Tragedy and Motive 192
    Reading: Analyze Causes and Effects 193
    Vocabulary Builder 194
    Conventions: Parallelism 195
    Support for Writing to Sources: Argumentative Text 196
    Support for Writing to Sources: Persuasive Speech 197
    Support for Speaking and Listening: Staged Performance; Mock Trial 198
    Support for Research and Technology: Presentation of Ideas 199

Comparing Texts: "Pyramus and Thisbe" by Ovid, The Tragedy of Romeo and Juliet by William Shakespeare, and *from* A Midsummer Night's Dream by William Shakespeare
    Writing About the Big Question 200
    Literary Analysis: Archetypal Themes—Ill-fated Love 201
    Vocabulary Builder 202
    Support for Writing to Sources: Explanatory Essay 203

Writing Process 204
Writer's Toolbox: Conventions 205

UNIT 4 • PART 3 Developing Insights

from **The Importance Being Earnest by Oscar Wilde**
    Vocabulary Builder 206
    Take Notes for Discussion 207
    Take Notes for Writing to Sources 208
    Take Notes for Research 209

"The Necklace" by Guy de Maupassant
    Vocabulary Builder 210
    Take Notes for Discussion 211
    Take Notes for Research 212
    Take Notes for Writing 213

"New Directions" by Maya Angelou
- Vocabulary Builder 214
- Take Notes for Discussion 215
- Take Notes for Research 216
- Take Notes for Writing to Sources 217

from "Fragile Self-Worth" by Tim Kasser
- Vocabulary Builder 218
- Take Notes for Discussion 219
- Take Notes for Research 220
- Take Notes for Writing to Sources 221

"My Possessions Myself" by Russell W. Belk
- Vocabulary Builder 222
- Take Notes for Discussion 223
- Take Notes for Research 224
- Take Notes for Writing to Sources 225

Cartoon from The New Yorker
- Vocabulary Builder and Take Notes for Writing to Sources 226

UNIT 5 • PART 1 Setting Expectations
- Big Question Vocabulary 1 227
- Big Question Vocabulary 2 228
- Big Question Vocabulary 3 229
- Applying the Big Question 230

UNIT 5 • PART 2 Guided Exploration

from The Odyssey, Part 1, by Homer
- Writing About the Big Question 231
- Literary Analysis: Epic Hero 232
- Reading: Analyze the Influence of Historical and Cultural Context 233
- Vocabulary Builder 234
- Conventions: Simple and Compound Sentences 235
- Support for Writing to Sources: Narrative Text (Retelling) 236
- Support for Speaking and Listening: Conversation 237

from The Odyssey, Part 2, by Homer
- Writing About the Big Question 238
- Literary Analysis: Epic Simile 239

Reading: Analyze the Influence of Historical and Cultural Context 240
Vocabulary Builder. 241
Conventions: Complex and Compound-Complex Sentences 242
Support for Writing to Sources: Informative Text (Biography) 243
Support for Speaking and Listening: Debate 244

**Comparing Texts: Poetry by Edna St. Vincent Millay,
Margaret Atwood, Derek Walcott, and Constantine Cavafy**
Writing About the Big Question 245
Literary Analysis: Contemporary Interpretations 246
Vocabulary Builder. 247
Support for Writing to Sources: Explanatory Text 248

Writing Process 249
Writer's Toolbox: Conventions 250

UNIT 5 • PART 3 Developing Insights
from The Ramayana, retold by R. K. Narayan
Vocabulary Builder. 251
Take Notes for Discussion 252
Take Notes for Writing to Sources 253
Take Notes for Research 254

"Perseus" by Edith Hamilton
Vocabulary Builder. 255
Take Notes for Discussion 256
Take Notes for Research 257
Take Notes for Writing to Sources 258

"The Washwoman" by Isaac Bashevis Singer
Vocabulary Builder. 259
Take Notes for Discussion 260
Take Notes for Research 261
Take Notes for Writing to Sources 262

from "The Hero's Adventure" by Joseph Campbell and Bill Moyers
Vocabulary Builder. 263
Take Notes for Discussion 264
Take Notes for Research 265
Take Notes for Writing to Sources 266

from **My Hero: Extraordinary People on the Heroes Who Inspire Them**
by Elie Wiesel
- Vocabulary Builder..267
- Take Notes for Discussion...268
- Take Notes for Research...269
- Take Notes for Writing to Sources................................270

"Of Altruism, Heroism and Nature's Gifts in the Face of Terror"
by Natalie Angier
- Vocabulary Builder..271
- Take Notes for Discussion...272
- Take Notes for Research...273
- Take Notes for Writing to Sources................................274

American Blood Donation
- Vocabulary Builder and Take Notes for Writing to Sources.......275

Unit 1: Short Stories
Big Question Vocabulary—1

The Big Question: Is conflict necessary?

When conflicts are discussed in a friendly, constructive way, sometimes we may begin to see the other side and to learn something.

amicably: acting in a friendly or peaceful way

appreciate: to understand how important or valuable something is

argument: a situation in which people disagree, often angrily

articulate: to express what you are thinking or feeling

differences: disagreements or controversies

DIRECTIONS: *Think of or invent a conflict that got resolved in a positive way. Write each step of the conflict using the vocabulary words. (For example, Step I could be Jason and I **argued** because he was late and kept me waiting.)*

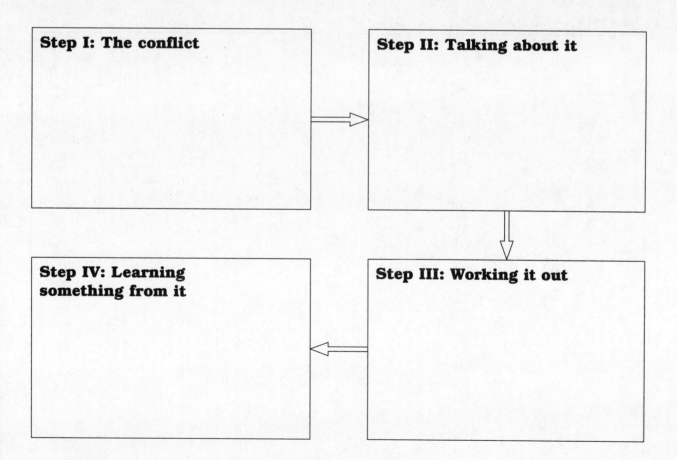

Name _____ Date _____

Unit 1: Short Stories
Big Question Vocabulary—2

The Big Question: Is conflict necessary?

Sometimes the actions of others can annoy or upset us. Some people have trouble expressing their displeasure in a constructive way. It is worth practicing this skill—working out differences in a productive way leads to a better atmosphere for everyone.

antagonize: to act in a way that annoys others; to act in opposition

compete: to try to be better or more successful than someone else

cooperate: to work together toward a common goal

grievance: a belief that you have been treated unfairly; a complaint about an unfair situation

mediate: to try to resolve or settle a conflict

DIRECTIONS: *Use the space below to write to someone who can help you resolve a complaint that you have. It can be real or imagined. Use all of the vocabulary words in your note.*

Unit 1: Short Stories
Big Question Vocabulary—3

 The Big Question: Is conflict necessary?

battle: a fight or competition between people or groups in which each side has the goal of winning

controversy: a serious argument about something that continues for a long time

equity: the state or quality of being fair and impartial

issue: a problem or topic that people discuss, especially a topic that affects a lot of people

survival: the state of continuing to exist where there is a risk of death

DIRECTIONS: *Use all of the vocabulary words to write a newspaper article describing what happened at Gesco Inc. after this sign was posted for all employees to see.*

Notice to All Employees

It is everyone's responsibility to help the homeless. Therefore, Gesco Inc. will be deducting 10% of the pay of each employee to donate to the homeless.
Thank you.

Trouble at Gesco Inc.

Name _____ Date _____

Unit 1: Short Stories
Applying the Big Question

 The Big Question: Is conflict necessary?

DIRECTIONS: Complete the chart below to apply what you have learned about conflict and whether or not it is necessary. One row has been completed for you.

Example	Conflict	Outcome	Was the Conflict Necessary for the Outcome?	What I Learned
From Literature	In "The Most Dangerous Game," one hunter forces another to be hunted as game.	The man who was forced to participate proves victorious.	Yes, because it forced the two men to **battle.**	A conflict can focus on **survival.**
From Literature				
From Science				
From Social Studies				
From Real Life				

All-in-One Workbook
© Pearson Education, Inc. All rights reserved.

Name _____   Date _____

"The Most Dangerous Game" by Richard Connell
Writing About the Big Question

Is conflict necessary?

Big Question Vocabulary

amicably	antagonize	appreciate	argument	articulate
compete/competition	controversy	cooperate	differences	equity
grievance	issue	mediate	survival	war/battle

A. *Use one or more words from the list above to complete each sentence.*

1. When Kim and her parents came to an agreement about her curfew, they resolved the conflict _____.

2. After Joe and Mark talked about a pressing political _____, they realized they had big _____ of opinion.

3. Todd and José built a model volcano to _____ in the science fair.

B. *Follow the directions in responding to each item below.*

1. Write two sentences describing a grievance you have had.
   _____
   _____

2. Write two sentences explaining how you dealt with the grievance. Use at least two of the Big Question vocabulary words.
   _____
   _____

C. In "The Most Dangerous Game," a hunter faces a life-threatening conflict. Complete the sentence below. Then, write a short paragraph in which you connect this experience to the Big Question.

To succeed in a fight for survival, a person needs to _____
_____
_____
_____

Name _____ Date _____

"The Most Dangerous Game" by Richard Connell
Literary Analysis: Conflict

Conflict is a struggle between opposing forces. There are two types of conflict: internal and external.

- In **internal conflict,** a character struggles with his or her own opposing feelings, beliefs, needs, or desires.
- In **external conflict,** a character struggles against an outside force, such as another character, society, or nature.

Conflict and the search for a solution are the mainspring of a story's plot. The solution, which usually occurs near the end of a story, is called the **resolution.** In some stories, the conflict is not truly resolved. Instead, the main character experiences an **epiphany,** or sudden flash of insight. Although the conflict is not resolved, the character's thoughts about it change.

A. DIRECTIONS: *"The Most Dangerous Game" contains a number of conflicts. On the following lines, briefly describe the story situations surrounding each conflict.*

1. Rainsford vs. nature _____
   _____
   _____

2. General Zaroff vs. the "visitors" to his island _____
   _____
   _____

3. Rainsford vs. General Zaroff _____
   _____
   _____

4. Rainsford within himself _____
   _____
   _____

B. DIRECTIONS: *On the following lines, briefly discuss the story's ending. Does the ending contain a resolution that solves the story's main conflict? Have Rainsford's experiences changed his views about hunting? Explain your answer by citing details from the story.*

_____
_____
_____
_____
_____
_____

Name _____ Date _____

"The Most Dangerous Game" by Richard Connell
Reading: Use Details to Make Inferences

An **inference** is a logical guess that you make based on details in a story. When you make inferences, you read between the lines to understand information that is not stated directly. To make inferences, ask yourself questions about the feelings and behavior of the characters. Here are some helpful questions to ask:

- What does this detail show about a character's motivation, or the reasons for his or her behavior?
- What does this passage say about the character's unspoken feelings and thoughts?

Example from "The Most Dangerous Game":

Detail from the story: "I can't believe you are serious, General Zaroff. This is a grisly joke."

Inference: Rainsford has just begun to realize that Zaroff hunts humans.

A. DIRECTIONS: *Use the following chart to make inferences from the details listed. The first item has been done for you.*

Details in the Story	My Inferences About Motivations/Feelings
1. Rainsford tells Whitney that there are only two classes of people: hunters and huntees.	Rainsford begins the story with a matter-of-fact, almost hard-boiled attitude.
2. Rainsford asks Zaroff to excuse him for the night because he feels sick.	
3. Zaroff tells Rainsford how upset he was at the death of his dog Lazarus.	
4. Rainsford is able to rig up several ingenious traps, such as the Burmese tiger pit and a Malay mancatcher.	

B. DIRECTIONS: *Do you think "The Most Dangerous Game" has a serious theme, or message about human nature or behavior? Or, is it primarily a suspenseful adventure story intended to entertain readers rather than to make a point? Explain your answer with specific references to details in the story.*

_____
_____
_____
_____
_____
_____
_____

Name _____ Date _____

"The Most Dangerous Game" by Richard Connell
Vocabulary Builder

Word List

futile   grotesque   indolently   naive   palpable   scruples

A. DIRECTIONS: *In each of the following items, think about the meaning of the italicized word, and then answer the question.*

1. What is the danger if you approach a research paper assignment *indolently*?
   _____
   _____

2. How are you feeling if you have *scruples* about doing something?
   _____
   _____

3. How would you feel if you make a long and *futile* journey?
   _____

4. If the tension during the final two minutes of a game is *palpable*, do you think the spectators feel suspense or not? Explain.
   _____

5. What is another word that can be used to describe something that is *grotesque*?
   _____

6. Is it *naive* to expect that starting a new business would be easy?
   _____

B. WORD STUDY: The Latin suffix *-esque* means "in the style or manner of." Use the context of the sentences and what you know about the **Latin suffix -esque** to explain your answer to each question.

1. Who directly influenced *Romanesque* architecture?
   _____

2. Is calling someone *statuesque* a compliment? Explain.
   _____

Name _____   Date _____

"The Most Dangerous Game" by Richard Connell
Conventions: Parts of Speech

English words are divided into categories, or **parts of speech**, based on how the words function in a sentence or phrase. There are eight parts of speech: **nouns (including proper nouns), pronouns, verbs, adjectives, adverbs, prepositions, conjunctions,** and **interjections**. This chart shows how some of them are used in sentences.

noun	names person, place, or thing	*Lyle* explored the *jungles* of the *Amazon*.
pronoun	takes the place of a noun or another pronoun	*He* watched for the deadly piranhas that inhabit the river and avoided *them*.
verb	describes an action	Lyle *explores* exotic regions and *collects* tropical plants.
adjective	modifies a noun or pronoun	The *mighty* Amazon is the *widest* river in the world.
adverb	modifies a verb, adjective, or another adverb	The Amazon explorers chose their supplies *wisely* and packed them *very carefully*.
preposition	clarifies relationships of time, place, or direction among other words in a sentence	The explorers left *at* noon and canoed *up* the river, leaving civilization *behind* them.

A. PRACTICE: *Write the part of speech of the italicized word or words in each sentence.*

1. _____ The rain beat loudly *on* the tent.
2. _____ Cutting a *path* into the *jungle* was a hard *task*.
3. _____ A snake *slithered* away and *disappeared* in the underbrush.
4. _____ The men *quickly* loaded the truck and *then* continued their work.
5. _____ *At* nightfall, they returned *to* the canoe.

B. WRITING APPLICATION: Write a brief paragraph describing a jungle animal. In your paragraph, circle one example of each part of speech listed in the chart above. Write the part of speech above the circled word.

_____
_____
_____
_____

Name _____ Date _____

"The Most Dangerous Game" by Richard Connell
Support for Writing to Sources: Comparison-and-Contrast Essay

For your comparison-and-contrast essay, use the following chart to jot down notes to help you answer the questions.

Whitney	
Views About Hunting and Animals	**Supporting Details**

Rainsford	
Views About Hunting and Animals	**Supporting Details**

Zaroff	
Views About Hunting and Animals	**Supporting Details**

Name _____ Date _____

"The Most Dangerous Game" by Richard Connell
Support for Speaking and Listening: Oral Presentation

Use the lines below to help you prepare for giving an oral presentation. Research your subject using the Internet, newspapers, and other print sources. Consult your librarian for ideas of where to start.

Questions to be answered in your speech: _____

_____

_____

Game species to research: _____

_____

Key facts: _____

_____

_____

_____

Threats to these species: _____

_____

_____

Ideas for photos: _____

_____

Captions for photos: _____

_____

Name _____ Date _____

"The Gift of the Magi" by O. Henry
Writing About the Big Question

 Is conflict necessary?

Big Question Vocabulary

amicably	antagonize	appreciate	argument	articulate
compete/competition	controversy	cooperate	differences	equity
grievance	issue	mediate	survival	war/battle

A. *Use one or more words from the list above to complete each sentence.*

1. _____ about hot topics forms the basis of political debates.

2. If you _____ a person, you will likely end up in a conflict.

3. Sometimes it is necessary to engage in a(n) _____ .

4. The goal should be to resolve the problem _____ .

B. *Follow the directions in responding to each of the items below.*

1. Write two sentences describing a time when you entered a conflict.
   _____
   _____

2. Write two sentences about how you resolved that conflict. Use at least two of the Big Question vocabulary words.
   _____
   _____

C. *Complete the sentence below. Then, write a short paragraph in which you connect this experience to the Big Question.*

When money is tight, it is hard to show love because _____
_____
_____
_____
_____

Name _____ Date _____

"The Gift of the Magi" by O. Henry
Literary Analysis: Irony and Surprise Ending

Irony is a difference or a contradiction between appearance and reality or between what is expected and what actually happens.

- In **situational irony,** something happens in the story that directly contradicts the expectations of a character or the reader. For example, you would expect that if Jim works hard at his job for a year, he will get a raise. If he gets a pay cut instead, the situation is ironic.
- A **surprise ending** often helps to create situational irony through a turn of events that takes the reader by surprise. To make a surprise ending believable, the author builds clues into the story that make the ending logical.

A. DIRECTIONS: *For each of the following excerpts from "The Gift of the Magi," write **I** in the space provided if the excerpt is ironic. Write **N** if the excerpt is not ironic. On the lines following each item, briefly explain why the excerpt is or is not ironic.*

____ 1. "Tomorrow would be Christmas Day, and she had only $1.87 with which to buy Jim a present. She had been saving every penny she could for months, with this result."

_____
_____

____ 2. "Where she stopped the sign read: 'Mme. Sofronie. Hair Goods of All Kinds.' One flight up Della ran, and collected herself, panting. Madame, large, too white, chilly, hardly looked the 'Sofronie.'"

_____
_____

____ 3. "Grand as the watch was he sometimes looked at it on the sly on account of the old leather strap that he used in place of a chain."

_____
_____

____ 4. "They were expensive combs, she knew, and her heart had simply craved and yearned over them without the least hope of possession. And now they were hers, but the tresses that should have adorned the coveted adornments were gone."

_____
_____

B. DIRECTIONS: *On the following lines, briefly explain the surprise ending in "The Gift of the Magi." Then, explain how O. Henry makes the surprise ending seem logical.*

_____
_____
_____
_____

Name _____ Date _____

"The Gift of the Magi" by O. Henry
Reading: Use Prior Knowledge and Experience to Make Inferences

An **inference** is an educated guess that you make based on details in a text. In addition to what the author tells you, you can also **use your own prior knowledge and experience** to make inferences.

- As you read, watch movies and plays, and observe the world every day, you gather knowledge and experience.
- When you read something new, look for ways in which the characters and situations resemble ones you have seen before.
- Then, apply that knowledge and experience to make inferences about what you are reading.

Example from "The Gift of the Magi":

Detail from the story: "A furnished flat at $8 per week."

Inference: Della and Jim do not have much money. They have to scrimp and save to get by.

DIRECTIONS: *Use the following chart to record information about the characters listed. Then, make three more inferences about each character based on the details from the story. Some examples are shown.*

Details About Della	Inferences I Can Make About Della
1. She hugs Jim every time he comes home.	Della is deeply in love with her husband.
2. _____	_____
3. _____	_____

Details About Jim	Inferences I Can Make About Jim
1. He greatly values his watch, which was handed down to him.	He has strong feelings for his family.
2. _____	_____
3. _____	_____

All-in-One Workbook
© Pearson Education, Inc. All rights reserved.

Name _____ Date _____

"The Gift of the Magi" by O. Henry
Vocabulary Builder

Word List

cascade   depreciate   discreet   faltered   instigates   prudence

A. DIRECTIONS: *Decide whether each of the following statements is true or false, and write* **T** *or* **F** *on the line provided. Then, explain your answer.*

1. A person who *instigates* conflict might be called a "problem solver." _____
_____

2. A car's value will *depreciate* after six years of hard use. _____
_____

3. Only a *discreet* person should be trusted with a secret. _____
_____

4. If a person *faltered*, he or she is likely confident. _____
_____

5. A person who practices *prudence* spends a lot of money. _____
_____

6. A waterfall can be described as a *cascade*. _____
_____

B. WORD STUDY: The prefix *de-* means "down." Use the context of the sentences and what you know about the **Latin prefix *de-*** to explain your answer to each question.

1. If you were to *devalue* a house, what would you do to it?
_____

2. What happens if a king is *deposed*?
_____

Name _____ Date _____

"The Gift of the Magi" by O. Henry
Conventions: Simple and Perfect Tenses

Verb tenses, or forms, tell when something happened or existed. English verbs have six different tenses:

Simple Tenses:

- Present indicates an action that happens regularly or states a general truth: *I practice the piano every day for my upcoming recital.*
- Past indicates an action that has already happened: *Yesterday, I practiced for two hours.*
- Future indicates an action that will happen: *I will practice even longer tomorrow.*

Perfect Tenses:

- Present Perfect indicates an action that happened at some time in the past or an action that happened in the past and is still happening now: *I have practiced for a month without missing a day.*
- Past Perfect indicates an action that was completed before another action in the past: *My teacher said I had practiced too little for last year's recital.*
- Future Perfect indicates an action that will have been completed before another: *By the time of the recital, I will have practiced more than one hundred hours.*

A. Practice: *On the line provided, write the tense of the verb in italics.*

1. Della *counted* her money.
   _____

2. She *had saved* too little for a gift.
   _____

3. She *will get* more money in exchange for her hair.
   _____

B. Writing Application: *Rewrite these sentences using the verb and tense in parentheses.*

4. Jim (own) a valuable watch. (past)
   _____

5. He (obtain) money from the sale of his watch. (present perfect)
   _____

6. He (use) the money for combs for Della. (future)
   _____

Name _____ Date _____

"The Gift of the Magi" by O. Henry
Writing to Sources: Narrative Text (News Report)

To gather information for your brief news report, use the following graphic organizer. Jot down some notes that answer the six questions that reporters ask: *Who? What? When? Where? Why? How?*

Questions	Answers
Who?	
What?	
When?	
Where?	
Why?	
How?	

Use the most important, eye-catching details in your notes to write the lead (opening) paragraph of your human-interest news story on the following lines.

_____
_____
_____
_____
_____
_____
_____

On a separate piece of paper, write your revised lead paragraph and choose other details to write the remaining paragraphs of your story.

Name _____ Date _____

"**The Gift of the Magi**" by O. Henry
Support for Speaking and Listening: Debate

Use the following lines to gather information for your debate about the lesson of "The Gift of the Magi." Under each debate position, list some quotations from the story to support that position.

POSITION 1: The story's lesson is that it is foolish to spend money on gifts instead of necessities.

Support for this position:

Example: "Twenty dollars a week doesn't go far. Expenses had been greater than she had calculated. They always are."

_____
_____
_____
_____
_____

POSITION 2: The story's lesson is that sacrifice is the best expression of love.

Support for this position:

Example: "'Will you buy my hair?' asked Della."

_____
_____
_____
_____
_____

Name _____ Date _____

"Rules of the Game" by Amy Tan
Writing About the Big Question

 Is conflict necessary?

Big Question Vocabulary

amicably	antagonize	appreciate	argument	articulate
compete/competition	controversy	cooperate	differences	equity
grievance	issue	mediate	survival	war/battle

A. *Use one or more words from the list above to complete each sentence.*

1. Because Mrs. March had no bias, she was able to deal with the students' conflict with _____.

2. The team's _____ for the league championship was challenging.

3. After Amanda explained how she felt, Kyle said, "I _____ your honesty."

4. _____ in the woods without modern conveniences was the goal of the scouts' camping trip.

B. *Follow the directions in responding to each of the items below.*

1. Describe a conflict you were able to mediate with equity.
   _____
   _____

2. Articulate your opinion about a current event or issue.
   _____
   _____

C. *Complete the sentence below. Then, write a short paragraph in which you connect this experience to the Big Question.*

Competition can cause internal conflict because _____
_____
_____
_____

All-in-One Workbook

Name _____ Date _____

"Rules of the Game" by Amy Tan
Literary Analysis: Character and Characterization

A **character** is a person, an animal, or even an object that participates in the action and experiences the events of a literary work. Writers communicate what characters are like through **characterization.** There are two main types of characterization:

- **Direct characterization:** The writer tells readers what a character is like.
- **Indirect characterization:** The writer gives readers clues to a character. The writer might show the character's behavior, present the character's words and thoughts, describe the character's physical appearance, or reveal what other characters say or think about the character. Often when a writer uses indirect characterization, it is up to the reader to draw logical conclusions about the character's personality and motivations.

The next week I bit back my tongue as we entered the store with the forbidden candies. When my mother finished her shopping, she quietly plucked a small bag of plums from the rack and put it on the counter with the rest of the items.

In this example, we get a glimpse of the characters' personalities through their actions. Meimei's mother rewards her for learning the secret of invisible strength and biting back her tongue.

DIRECTIONS: *On the lines provided, briefly explain how each excerpt from the story helps to characterize one or more of the characters.*

1. My mother imparted her daily truths so she could help my older brothers and me rise above our circumstances.
   _____
   _____

2. When we got home, my mother told Vincent to throw the chess set away. "She not want it. We not want it," she said, tossing her head stiffly to the side with a tight, proud smile.
   _____
   _____

3. At the next tournament, I won again, but it was my mother who wore the triumphant grin. "Lost eight piece this time. Last time was eleven. What I tell you? Better off less!" I was annoyed, but I couldn't say anything.
   _____
   _____

4. My mother would proudly walk with me, visiting many shops, buying very little. "This my daughter Wave-ly Jong," she said to whoever looked her way.
   _____
   _____

Name _____ Date _____

"Rules of the Game" by Amy Tan
Reading: Ask Questions to Analyze Cause and Effect

A **cause** is an event, action, or feeling that produces a result. An **effect** is the result produced. As you read, **ask questions to analyze cause and effect.** Examining these relationships helps you follow the logic that moves a story forward. As you read, ask yourself the following questions:

- What happened?
- Why did it happen?
- What happens as a result?

A single cause may produce several effects. For example, a character who is saving to buy a bicycle takes a baby-sitting job with her neighbor's children. This leads to her starting a summer play group and starts her thinking about getting a college degree in early childhood education.

Effects may, in turn, become causes. That same character's successful experiences with young children leads her to volunteer on the pediatric floor of a local hospital.

DIRECTIONS: Use the cause-and-effect chart below to keep track of events in "Rules of the Game."

Cause	Effect
1. The Jong family goes to a church Christmas party.	Vincent gets a secondhand chess set.
2. Vincent and Winston play chess a lot.	
3.	
4.	
5.	
6.	
7.	

Name _____ Date _____

"Rules of the Game" by Amy Tan
Vocabulary Builder

Word List

    benevolently   concessions   malodorous   prodigy   pungent   retort

A. DIRECTIONS: *In each item below, think about the meaning of the italicized word, and then answer the question in a complete sentence.*

1. If a dish tastes *pungent*, is it spicy or bland? _____
_____

2. If you reply to a person with a *retort*, are you speaking sweetly or sharply? _____
_____

3. You enter a restaurant and notice that the air is *malodorous*. Explain whether or not you would choose to eat there. _____
_____

4. Would you feel happy if a classmate looked at you *benevolently*? Explain. _____
_____

5. Would a *prodigy* likely excel or fail? Explain. _____
_____

6. Are *concessions* given to help or hurt a person? Explain. _____
_____

B. WORD STUDY: The root *-bene-* means "good" or "well." Use the context of the sentences and what you know about the **Latin root *-bene-*** to explain your answer to each question.

1. Would a charity appreciate a *benefaction*? Why?
_____
_____

2. How is studying for an exam *beneficial*?
_____
_____

Name _____ Date _____

"Rules of the Game" by Amy Tan
Conventions: Subjects and Predicates

Every sentence is made of two parts, a subject and a predicate. The **complete subject** includes all the words that tell whom or what a sentence is about. The **complete predicate** includes all the words that tell what the subject of a sentence does or is. The **simple subject** and **simple predicate,** underlined below, are the noun and verb that make a sentence complete. A subject and its verb should always agree in number.

Complete Subject	Complete Predicate
Setting up the chess board, her <u>brothers</u>	<u>prepared</u> to play.
Many curious <u>people</u>	<u>gather</u> to watch Waverly play chess.

A. DIRECTIONS: *Draw a vertical line in each sentence to separate the complete subject from the complete predicate.*

1. Amy Tan wrote "Rules of the Game."
2. Writing her story, Tan describes life on Waverly Place.
3. The alley on Waverly Place was crammed with adventures.
4. Waverly, the narrator, watched her brothers' chess games.
5. The eager young girl borrowed books to research the rules of the game.
6. Walking home from school, Waverly stopped to play chess with an old man.

B. DIRECTIONS: *Write one sentence on each of the lines below about the life described in "The Rules of the Game." For each sentence, draw a vertical line between the complete subject and the complete predicate. Then, underline the simple subject and the simple predicate.*

1. _____
2. _____
3. _____
4. _____
5. _____

All-in-One Workbook

Name _____ Date _____

"Rules of the Game" by Amy Tan
Support for Writing to Sources: Informative Text

Use the lines below to jot down notes about the issues the characters face and your suggestions for resolving them.

Issue 1: _____
_____

My suggestions on how to resolve this issue: _____
_____
_____
_____

Issue 2: _____
_____

My suggestions on how to resolve this issue: _____
_____
_____
_____

Issue 3: _____
_____

My suggestions on how to resolve this issue: _____
_____
_____
_____

Issue 4: _____
_____

My suggestions on how to resolve this issue: _____
_____
_____
_____

Now, use your notes to write your written presentation. Make a special effort not to favor one character over the other. Keep your tone neutral, and revise any language that sounds biased in favor of one of the characters.

All-in-One Workbook
© Pearson Education, Inc. All rights reserved.

Name _____ Date _____

"Rules of the Game" by Amy Tan
Support for Research and Technology: Informative Brochure

Use the lines below to make notes for your informative brochure about how to play chess.

1. Description of chess board and pieces _____
   _____
   _____

2. How each piece moves _____
   _____
   _____
   _____

3. How play begins _____
   _____

4. How the game ends _____
   _____

5. What is a draw? _____
   _____

Sources

1. _____
   _____

2. _____
   _____

3. _____
   _____

"The Cask of Amontillado" by Edgar Allan Poe
Writing About the Big Question

...ict necessary?

Big Question Vocabulary

amicably	antagonize	appreciate	argument	articulate
compete/competition	controversy	cooperate	differences	equity
grievance	issue	mediate	survival	war/battle

A. Use one or more words from the list above to complete each sentence.

1. Alice and Cyrus argued about a topic for their history project, but they resolved their conflict _____.

2. When Ana and Jay disagreed over a Student Council _____, they realized they had big _____ of opinion.

3. Lana and Jen both harbored a wish to _____ in the district track meet.

B. Follow the directions in responding to each item below.

1. Write two sentences describing a grievance you have had.
   _____
   _____

2. Write two sentences explaining how you dealt with the grievance. Use at least two of the Big Question vocabulary words.
   _____
   _____

C. In "The Cask of Amontillado," the narrator has a grievance against Fortunato. Complete the sentence below. Then, write a short paragraph in which you connect this experience to the Big Question.

To settle an old grievance against someone, a person needs to _____
_____
_____
_____

All-in-One Workbook
© Pearson Education, Inc. All rights reserved.

Name _____ Date _____

"The Cask of Amontillado" by Edgar Allan Poe
Literary Analysis: Plot, Foreshadowing, and Suspense

Plot is the sequence of events in a narrative. It is structured around a **conflict,** or problem, and it can be divided into the following parts:

- **Exposition**—the characters and setting are introduced
- **Rising action**—the central conflict is introduced
- **Climax**—the high point of intensity in the conflict
- **Falling action**—the conflict's intensity lessens
- **Resolution**—the conflict concludes and loose ends are tied up

Writers use a variety of techniques to keep readers interested in the plot. One of these, **foreshadowing,** is the use of clues to hint at events that will happen later in a story. Authors use this technique to create **suspense,** a feeling of tension that keeps readers wondering what will happen next.

Read the following passage, which is the opening paragraph of "The Cask of Amontillado."

> The thousand injuries of Fortunato I had borne as I best could, but when he ventured upon insult I vowed revenge. You, who so well know the nature of my soul, will not suppose, however, that I gave utterance to a threat. At *length* I would be avenged; this was a point definitely settled—but the very definitiveness with which it was resolved precluded the idea of risk. I must not only punish but punish with impunity.

In the opening paragraph, what details does Poe include that suggest something about the narrator's personality and his plans? The paragraph arouses our curiosity: What does the narrator plan to do, and how can he possibly get away without being punished?

A. DIRECTIONS: *Read the following passage, and watch for details the author uses to create suspense. Underline the words and phrases in the passage that make you curious about the outcome.*

> The wine sparkled in his eyes and the bells jingled. My own fancy grew warm with the Médoc. We had passed through long walls of piled skeletons, with casks and puncheons intermingling, into the inmost recesses of the catacombs. I paused again, and this time I made bold to seize Fortunato by an arm above the elbow.
>
> "The niter!" I said; "see, it increases. It hangs like moss upon the vaults. We are below the river's bed. The drops of moisture trickle among the bones. Come, we will go back ere it is too late. Your cough—"
>
> "It is nothing," he said; "let us go on. But first, another draft of the Médoc."

B. DIRECTIONS: *Identify two clues the author gives that foreshadow the story's ending. Did you expect the story's ending, or were you surprised? Describe your response, and tell why you reacted that way.*

Clue 1: _____

Clue 2: _____

My response to story's ending: _____

_____

Name _____ Date _____

"The Cask of Amontillado" by Edgar Allan Poe
Reading: Read Ahead to Make and Verify Predictions

A **prediction** is an informed guess about what will happen later in a narrative. **Making and verifying predictions** keeps you actively involved in the story you are reading.

- Notice details that may foreshadow future events. Make predictions based on those details, and then read on to verify your predictions. If a prediction turns out to be wrong, evaluate your reasoning to determine whether you misread details or whether the author purposely created false expectations in order to surprise you later in the story.
- Use a chart like the one shown to record your predictions and evaluate their accuracy. Analyze any inaccurate predictions to determine why they were incorrect.

The key to making accurate predictions is paying close attention to the story's details as you read. In "The Cask of Amontillado," the author provides many colorful details that serve as hints about what will happen.

Poe's original: I took from their sconces two flambeaux, and giving one to Fortunato, bowed him through several suites of rooms to the archway that led into the vaults. I passed down a long and winding staircase, requesting him to be cautious as he followed. We came at length to the foot of the descent, and stood together upon the damp ground of the catacombs of the Montresors.

Prediction: The narrator is going to do something terrible to Fortunato in the catacombs.

DIRECTIONS: *Fill in the columns on the following chart. In the second column, write your prediction based on the details in the first column. Then, read ahead to find out the outcome. How closely did your predictions match the outcomes? Record the outcomes in the third column.*

Details	My Prediction	Outcome
1. "Thus speaking, Fortunato possessed himself of my arm; and putting on a mask of black silk and drawing a roquelaure closely about my person, I suffered him to hurry me to my palazzo."		
2. "There were no attendants at home; they had absconded to make merry in honor of the time."		
3. It was in vain that Fortunato, uplifting his dull torch, endeavored to pry into the depth of the recess. Its termination the feeble light did not enable us to see. "Proceed," I said: "herein is the Amontillado...."		

Name _____ Date _____

"The Cask of Amontillado" by Edgar Allan Poe
Vocabulary Builder

Word List

afflicted   explicit   precluded   recoiling   retribution   subsided

A. DIRECTIONS: *Write the letter of the word that is most nearly* opposite *in meaning to the Word List word.*

___ 1. precluded
    A. allowed   B. prevented   C. discouraged   D. interrupted

___ 2. retribution
    A. punishment   B. reward   C. criticism   D. response

___ 3. explicit
    A. distinct   B. clear   C. complete   D. vague

___ 4. afflicted
    A. invigorated   B. confused   C. sickened   D. worried

___ 5. recoiling
    A. retreating   B. forgetting   C. lurching   D. advancing

___ 6. subsided
    A. weakened   B. relaxed   C. intensified   D. begun

B. WORD STUDY The suffix *-tion* means "the act of." Rewrite each sentence. Use the underlined word plus the suffix *-tion* in the new sentence.

1. As I walked up the mountain, the trail began to elevate more and more.
   _____

2. The huge male lion will protect the rest of the group.
   _____

3. When he could not pay his rent, the landlord threatened to evict him.
   _____

4. The coach sent in a substitute player when John was injured.
   _____

"The Cask of Amontillado" by Edgar Allan Poe
Conventions: Active Voice and Passive Voice

Active and Passive Voice

A verb in the **active voice** expresses an action done *by* its subject.
  Edgar Allan Poe *created* that famous story.

A verb in the **passive voice** expresses an action done *to* its subject.
  That famous story *was created* by Edgar Allan Poe.

A. DIRECTIONS: *Underline the verb or verbs in each sentence. Tell whether each is in the active or passive voice.*

1. Fortunato drank too much wine.

2. The bottle was emptied quickly.

3. Fortunato leaned on my arm.

4. The crypt was filled with a damp, musty odor.

5. Its walls had been lined with human remains.

B. DIRECTIONS: *Write a paragraph describing the character of the narrator. Use verbs in both the active voice and the passive voice. Underline the verbs and then write "A" or "P" above each verb to show whether it is active or passive voice.*

Name _____ Date _____

"The Cask of Amontillado" by Edgar Allan Poe
Support for Writing to Sources: Argumentative Text

Use the following chart to list the qualities that make a story suspenseful and that make the ending of a story satisfactory. Then, put a check mark in front of the qualities that you think apply to "The Cask of Amontillado."

Qualities That Make a Story Suspenseful	Qualities of a Satisfactory Ending
❑ _____	❑ _____
❑ _____	❑ _____
❑ _____	❑ _____
❑ _____	❑ _____
❑ _____	❑ _____
❑ _____	❑ _____

Now, use your notes to write your critique in which you evaluate the ending of "The Cask of Amontillado."

Name _____ Date _____

"The Cask of Amontillado" by Edgar Allan Poe
Support for Speaking and Listening: Retelling

DIRECTIONS: *Plan your retelling of the story by answering the following questions.*

1. From whose point of view will you retell the story?
   _____

2. What facial expressions will you use? Describe two facial expressions and the specific lines you will be saying as you use each expression.

   Expression: _____

   What I will be saying: _____

   Expression: _____

   What I will be saying: _____

3. What body movements, or gestures, will you use? Describe two body movements and the specific lines you will be saying as you use each body movement.

   Body movement: _____

   What I will be saying: _____

   Body movement: _____

   What I will be saying: _____

4. Where in the story will I change my intonation and voice to reflect the emotions of the narrator? List four situations that call for changes in voice. Describe your intonation and voice for each.

   a. _____
      _____

   b. _____
      _____

   c. _____
      _____

   d. _____
      _____

Name _____ Date _____

"**Checkouts**" by Cynthia Rylant
"**The Girl Who Can**" by Ama Ata Aidoo

Writing About the Big Question

Is conflict necessary?

Big Question Vocabulary

amicably	antagonize	appreciate	argument	articulate
compete/competition	controversy	cooperate	differences	equity
grievance	issue	mediate	survival	war/battle

A. *Use one or more words from the list above to complete each sentence.*

1. The checkout boy was unable to _____ his feelings.
2. Nana and Maami had been able to _____ the importance of school.
3. Nana was very proud that her granddaughter had won the _____.

B. *Follow the directions in responding to each item below.*

1. Write two sentences describing a controversy about the expense of sports programs.
   _____
   _____

2. Write two sentences describing the differences in opinion that sparked the controversy. Use at least two Big Question Vocabulary Words in your sentences.
   _____
   _____

C. *In "The Girl Who Can," the author describes the conflict between traditional ideas about girls and the desires of a young girl. Complete the sentences below. Then, write a short paragraph in which you connect this experience to the Big Question.*

The modern world sometimes conflicts with traditional ways because _____
_____
_____

When these differences can be resolved, _____
_____
_____
_____

Name _____ Date _____

"Checkouts" by Cynthia Rylant
"The Girl Who Can" by Ama Ata Aidoo
Literary Analysis: Point of View

Point of view is the perspective from which a story is narrated, or told.

- **First-person point of view:** The narrator is a character who participates in the action of the story and uses the first-person pronouns *I* and *me*.
- **Third-person point of view:** The narrator is not a character in the story but is a voice outside the action. The narrator uses the third-person pronouns *he, she, him, her, they,* and *them* to refer to all characters. There are two kinds of third-person points of view. In the **third-person omniscient** point of view, the narrator knows everything, including the thoughts and feelings of all the characters. In the **third-person limited** point of view, the narrator sees the world through a single character's eyes and reveals that character's feelings and thoughts. The narrator can describe what other characters do or say but not what they feel or think.

A story's point of view affects what readers are told and what they must figure out. It may also affect which characters they identify or sympathize with and which characters they do not.

DIRECTIONS: *To understand point of view, readers must examine its effects on the telling of the story. It is sometimes useful to consider how a different point of view would affect the telling of the story. Answer the following questions to analyze the point of view in "Checkouts" and "The Girl Who Can."*

1. In "Checkouts," imagine that the author uses the first-person point of view with the girl as narrator. Review the description of the scene in which the bag boy drops and breaks the jar of mayonnaise. How would this scene be different if it were written from the first-person point of view?

   _____
   _____
   _____
   _____

2. Suppose that "The Girl Who Can" were told in the third-person omniscient point of view. Review the final scene in the story, in which Nana carries the trophy cup home on her back. How would this scene be different if it were told in the third-person omniscient point of view?

   _____
   _____
   _____
   _____
   _____
   _____

Name _____ Date _____

"Checkouts" by Cynthia Rylant
"The Girl Who Can" by Ama Ata Aidoo
Vocabulary Builder

Word List

comprehension   dishevelment   fertile   humble   perverse   reverie

A. DIRECTIONS: *Revise each sentence so that the underlined vocabulary word is used logically. Be sure not to change the vocabulary word.*

1. Sunk in <u>reverie</u>, the six-year-old twins had surprised expressions on their faces.
   _____

2. She brags endlessly about her accomplishments in a <u>humble</u> manner.
   _____

3. Hours of careful grooming resulted in Sam's state of <u>dishevelment</u> at the party.
   _____

4. May's sister took a <u>perverse</u> pleasure in making her laugh.
   _____

5. The soil is so extremely <u>fertile</u> that nothing can be grown in it.
   _____

B. DIRECTIONS: *Answer the following questions in the space provided.*

1. How would a person with a <u>humble</u> attitude behave?
   _____
   _____

2. Describe the appearance of a <u>fertile</u> piece of land.
   _____
   _____

3. How would you feel if you were sure of your <u>comprehension</u> of a complex topic?
   _____
   _____

Name _____ Date _____

"Checkouts" by Cynthia Rylant
"The Girl Who Can" by Ama Ata Aidoo
Support for Writing to Sources: Explanatory Text

Use a chart like the one below to make prewriting notes for your essay of comparison and contrast.

Points of Comparison/Contrast	"Checkouts"	"The Girl Who Can"
Who is the narrator in each story?		
What is the point of view?		
What do we learn of the thoughts and feelings of the girl and of Adjoa?		
How do other characters react to the girl and Adjoa?		

All-in-One Workbook
© Pearson Education, Inc. All rights reserved.

Name _____ Date _____

Writing Process
Argument: Response to Literature

Use the following note cards to gather evidence that supports your claims.

Thesis 1: What I Want to Prove:

How I can prove it:
_____
_____

Explain in detail:
_____
_____
_____

Thesis 2: What I Want to Prove:

How I can prove it:
_____
_____

Explain in detail:
_____
_____
_____

Thesis 3: What I Want to Prove:

How I can prove it:
_____
_____

Explain in detail:
_____
_____
_____

Name _____   Date _____

Writer's Toolbox
Conventions: Using Quotations

Using direct quotations from a text is an excellent way to provide support claims about a literary text. Be careful to punctuate direct and indirect quotations properly.

- **Punctuation for Direct Quotations**

Quotation marks: A quotation embedded in your writing should be enclosed in quotation marks, preceded by a comma or colon, and followed by a page number.

Jill expresses her happiness by saying, "This is the best day ever!" (23).

No quotation marks: Quotations that run longer than four lines in your text should be set off in a block of text that is indented ten spaces. Do not use quotation marks.

The setting of the story creates a somber mood:

> *The house was old and dilapidated. Shutters banged against the bricks with a forlorn clatter. Most of the windows were cracked and many were painted black, which gave the house an ominous look even during a day with bright sunshine. (42)*

- **Punctuation for Indirect Quotations**

No quotation marks: Because indirect quotations are not the exact words from a text, you do not enclose them in quotation marks and do not include a page number.

The house, with its dilapidated appearance and yard full of weeds, creates a somber mood.

A. DIRECTIONS: *Put a C in front of any sentence that has a direct or indirect quotation punctuated correctly. Put an I in front of any sentence that is punctuated incorrectly.*

_____ 1. The narrator reveals a surprise: "All of a sudden, Jim hit a home run!" (23).

_____ 2. Ellen said "that she would never give up" (22).

_____ 3. Sandra called out loudly, Watch out for that tree! (4).

_____ 4. When Joe gets home, he realizes his mistake.

B. WRITING APPLICATION: *On the lines provided, rewrite these sentences with correct punctuation. Use page numbers only for direct quotations.*

1. Many feel "that urban coyotes are a nuisance" (12).

   _____

2. Lia finally understands the situation: I will not run again (9).

   _____

3. The reader learns the truth when Mr. Capp whispers, I am the culprit (6).

   _____

4. Most readers "will think that the plot of the story is well developed."

   _____

Name _____ Date _____

"The Scarlet Ibis" by James Hurst
Vocabulary Builder

Selection Vocabulary

    imminent   infallibility   precariously

A. DIRECTIONS: *Complete each sentence with a phrase or clause that contains a context clue for the italicized word.*

1. The student knew that the climax of the story was *imminent* because _____
_____.

2. In a perfect world, everyone would have *infallibility,* but in the real world, everyone
_____

3. If a person is standing somewhere *precariously,* the best thing for him or her to do would be _____.

Academic Vocabulary

    detract   effective   pervade

B. DIRECTIONS: *Write a response to each question. Make sure to use the word in italics at least once in your response.*

1. What is an *effective* way to show the personality of a story character?
_____
_____

2. What quality in a character might *detract* from your appreciation of him or her? Explain.
_____

3. What mood might *pervade* a mystery story?
_____
_____

Name _____ Date _____

"The Scarlet Ibis" by James Hurst
Take Notes for Discussion

Before the Group Discussion: Read the following passage from the story.

> Once he could go no further, so he collapsed on the ground and began to cry.
> "Aw, come on, Doodle," I urged. "You can do it. Do you want to be different from everybody else when you start school?"
> "Does it make any difference?"
> "It certainly does," I said.

During the Discussion: As your group discusses each question, take notes on how other students' ideas either differ from or build upon your own.

Discussion Questions	Other Ideas Expressed	Comparison to My Own Ideas
1. Why do you think the narrator wants to change Doodle?		
2. Should Doodle try to be the same as other children? Why or why not?		
3. What motivates Doodle to try to change?		

Name _____ Date _____

"The Scarlet Ibis" by James Hurst
Take Notes for Writing to Sources

Planning Your Comparison and Contrast: Before you begin drafting your **comparison-and-contrast** essay, use the chart below to organize your ideas. The first column lists characteristics. Use the second column to jot down characteristics of the narrator, and use the third column to jot down characteristics of Doodle.

Characteristics	Characteristics of Narrator	Characteristics of Doodle
1. Appearance		
2. Behavior (actions, words, gestures, etc.)		
3. Thoughts and Feelings		
4. Motivations		

All-in-One Workbook

Name _____ Date _____

"The Scarlet Ibis" by James Hurst
Take Notes for Research

As you research the **ways in which people with physical or mental differences have been treated in various cultures or eras,** use the forms below to take notes from your sources. As necessary, continue your notes on the back of this page, on note cards, or in a word-processing document.

Source Information   Check one: ☐ Primary Source   ☐ Secondary Source

Title: _____ Author: _____

Publication Information: _____

Page(s): _____

Main Idea: _____

_____

Quotation or Paraphrase: _____

_____

Source Information   Check one: ☐ Primary Source   ☐ Secondary Source

Title: _____ Author: _____

Publication Information: _____

Page(s): _____

Main Idea: _____

_____

Quotation or Paraphrase: _____

_____

Source Information   Check one: ☐ Primary Source   ☐ Secondary Source

Title: _____ Author: _____

Publication Information: _____

Page(s): _____

Main Idea: _____

_____

Quotation or Paraphrase: _____

_____

Name _____ Date _____

"Much Madness is divinest sense" by Emily Dickinson
Vocabulary Builder

Selection Vocabulary

    discerning   prevail

A. Directions: *Decide whether each statement below is true or false. On the line before each item, write TRUE or FALSE. Then explain your answers.*

_____ 1. A *discerning* person would tend to make foolish choices.

_____ 2. A situation that *prevails* would probably not last very long.

Academic Vocabulary

    contradictory   emphasize

B. Directions: *Each sentence below features an italicized word. Explain whether each sentence makes sense, given the meaning of the italicized word. If it does not make sense, write a new sentence using the word correctly.*

1. To *emphasize* his main ideas, the teacher spoke in a low voice.

2. The two leaders presented *contradictory* views, showing clearly that they were in total agreement.

Name _____ Date _____

"My English" by Julia Alvarez
Vocabulary Builder

Selection Vocabulary

    accentuated   bilingual   enumerated

A. DIRECTIONS: *Write the letter of the word or phrase that is the best synonym for the italicized word.*

_____ 1. *bilingual*
- A. being confused
- B. having three languages
- C. using two languages
- D. learning new languages

_____ 2. *enumerated*
- A. listed
- B. created
- C. required
- D. forgot

_____ 3. *accentuated*
- A. estimated
- B. excited
- C. emphasized
- D. abbreviated

Academic Vocabulary

    barrier   illustrate   noteworthy

B. DIRECTIONS: *Write a response to each question. Make sure to use the word in italics at least once in your response.*

1. What would be an effective way for people to *illustrate* their interest in writing poetry?
   _____
   _____

2. What might make an author a *noteworthy* author?
   _____
   _____

3. What *barrier* might make it difficult for someone to make a speech before a large crowd?
   _____
   _____

Name _____ Date _____

"My English" by Julia Alvarez
Take Notes for Discussion

Before the Partner Discussion: Read the following passage from the story.

> I would bow my head, humiliated by the smiles and snickers of the American children around me. I grew insecure about Spanish. My native tongue was not quite so good as English, as if words like *columpio* were illegal immigrants trying to cross a border into another language. But Teacher's discerning grammar and vocabulary-patrol ears could tell and send them back.

During the Discussion: As you discuss each question, take notes on how your partner's ideas either differ from or build upon your own.

Discussion Questions	Other Ideas Expressed	Comparison to My Own Ideas
1. Why do you think Alvarez uses law-enforcement terms ("patrol"; "illegal") in this passage?		
2. What does this passage say about the power of language to bring people together or to separate them?		

Name _____ Date _____

"My English" by Julia Alvarez
Take Notes for Research

Take Notes: As you research the **language barrier faced by some immigrants coming to the United States,** use the forms below to take notes from your sources. As necessary, continue your notes on the back of this page, on note cards, or in a word-processing document.

Source Information   Check one: ☐ Primary Source   ☐ Secondary Source

Title: _____   Author: _____

Publication Information: _____

Page(s): _____

Main Idea: _____
_____

Quotation or Paraphrase: _____
_____

Source Information   Check one: ☐ Primary Source   ☐ Secondary Source

Title: _____   Author: _____

Publication Information: _____

Page(s): _____

Main Idea: _____
_____

Quotation or Paraphrase: _____
_____

Source Information   Check one: ☐ Primary Source   ☐ Secondary Source

Title: _____   Author: _____

Publication Information: _____

Page(s): _____

Main Idea: _____
_____

Quotation or Paraphrase: _____
_____

Name _____ Date _____

"My English" by Julia Alvarez
Take Notes for Writing to Sources

Planning Your Explanation: Before you begin drafting your **explanatory essay,** use the chart below to organize your ideas. Follow the directions at the top of each box.

1. Define the term *idiom*, and give an example from the story.
_____
_____
_____
_____

2. Explain how Alvarez felt about idioms as she learned English. Give examples from the story to support your explanation.
_____
_____
_____
_____
_____
_____

3. Explain why idioms are difficult for language learners. Give an example from the story to support your explanation.
_____
_____
_____
_____
_____

4. Plan your conclusion. Make connections between your analysis and Alvarez's experiences.
_____
_____
_____
_____
_____
_____

Name _____ Date _____

"The Case for Fitting In" by David Berreby
Vocabulary Builder

Selection Vocabulary

    credentials   prejudice   solidarity

A. DIRECTIONS: *Revise each sentence so that the italicized vocabulary word is used logically. Be sure not to change the vocabulary word.*

1. Because she wanted to be fair, she based most of her views on *prejudice*.
   _____.

2. The king prided himself on the *solidarity* of his people because they held so many different views.
   _____
   _____.

3. The reporters were required to hide their *credentials* before entering the event.
   _____
   _____.

Academic Vocabulary

    distinction   critical   consult

B. DIRECTIONS: *Write the letter of the word or phrase that is the best synonym for the italicized word.*

_____ 1. *distinction*

     A. difference   C. truthfulness

     B. direction   D. carelessness

_____ 2. *critical*

     A. dangerous   C. optional

     B. healthy   D. vital

_____ 3. *consult*

     A. hope for   C. demand

     B. refer to   D. deny

Name _____ Date _____

"The Case for Fitting In" by David Berreby
Take Notes for Discussion

Before the Partner Discussion: Read the following passage from the selection.

> This means that the subjects in the most famous "people are sheep" experiment were not sheep at all—they were human beings who largely stuck to their guns, but now and then went along with the group. Why? Because in getting along with other people, most decent people know, as Hodges and Geyer put it, the "importance of cooperation, tact and social solidarity in situations that are tense or difficult."

During the Discussion: As you discuss each question, take notes on how your partner's ideas either differ from or build upon your own.

Discussion Questions	Other Ideas Expressed	Comparison to My Own Ideas
1. Why do you think Berreby includes the expressions "people are sheep" and "stuck to their guns"?		
2. Is following others for the purposes of cooperation or solidarity the same thing as conformity?		

All-in-One Workbook
© Pearson Education, Inc. All rights reserved.

Name _____ Date _____

"The Case for Fitting In" by David Berreby
Take Notes for Research

Take Notes: As you research the **ethical controversy surrounding Stanley Milgram's experiment and methods,** you can use the organizer below to take notes from your sources. As necessary, continue your notes on the back of this page, on note cards, or in a word-processing document.

The Ethical Controversy Surrounding Milgram's Experiment and Methods

Main Idea _____

Quotation or Paraphrase _____
_____
_____
_____
_____

Source Information _____
_____
_____
_____
_____
_____

Main Idea _____

Quotation or Paraphrase _____
_____
_____
_____
_____

Source Information _____
_____
_____
_____
_____
_____

Main Idea _____

Quotation or Paraphrase _____
_____
_____
_____
_____

Source Information _____
_____
_____
_____
_____
_____

Main Idea _____

Quotation or Paraphrase _____
_____
_____
_____
_____

Source Information _____
_____
_____
_____
_____
_____

Name _____ Date _____

"The Case for Fitting In" by David Berreby
Take Notes for Writing to Sources

Planning Your Argument: Before you begin drafting your **argumentative essay,** use the chart below to organize your ideas. In the first box, circle *agree* or *disagree* and then give your reasons.

My Position: I agree/disagree that Americans are biased in favor of "lone wolves." Here are my reasons: _____ _____ _____ _____
My Evidence: 1. The types of people that Americans admire are: _____ _____   2. Here are examples of heroes. (They might include politicians, military leaders, and characters from other popular media.) _____ _____
My analysis of two or three of the above figures: (Tell what qualities they have that make them admired. Does each display moral superiority? Does each stand alone?) _____ _____ _____ _____
My Conclusion: (Summarize your ideas, clearly stating whether you agree or disagree with Berreby's point and briefly explaining why.) _____ _____ _____ _____ _____

Name _____ Date _____

"The Geeks Shall Inherit the Earth" by Alexandra Robbins
Vocabulary Builder

Selection Vocabulary

    allegedly   monotonous   squelching

A. *Decide whether each statement below is true or false. On the line before each item, write TRUE or FALSE. Then explain your answers.*

_____ 1. An *allegedly* great bargain may not be a bargain at all.

_____

_____ 2. A *monotonous* series of events would be thrilling to experience.

_____

_____ 3. An effective way of *squelching* a child's desire to play a musical instrument is to provide the child with lessons and support.

_____

Academic Vocabulary

    analyze   characterize   evidence

B. DIRECTIONS: *Provide an explanation for your answer to each question.*

1. Think of a fictional character that you admire. How would you *characterize* him or her?
_____
_____

2. What facts could be used as *evidence* to support the following statement? *The Earth is round.*
_____
_____

3. When you *analyze* a poem, what features might you examine?
_____
_____

Name _____ Date _____

"The Geeks Shall Inherit the Earth" by Alexandra Robbins
Take Notes for Discussion

Before the Group Discussion: Read the following passage from the selection.

> The students outside these walls are the kids who typically are not considered part of the in crowd, the ones who are excluded, blatantly or subtly, from the premier table in the lunchroom. I refer to them as "cafeteria fringe." Whether alone or in groups, these geeks, loners, punks, floaters, nerds, freaks, dorks, gamers, bandies, art kids, theater geeks, choir kids, Goths, weirdos, indies, scenes, emos, skaters, and various types of racial and other minorities are often relegated to subordinate social status simply because they are, or seem to be, even the slightest bit different.

During the Discussion: As you discuss each question, take notes on how other students' ideas either differ from or build upon your own.

Discussion Questions	Other Ideas Expressed	Comparison to My Own Ideas
1. What does the list of "cafeteria fringe" students suggest about the group?		
2. Should the students on this list be encouraged to conform? Why or why not?		

All-in-One Workbook
© Pearson Education, Inc. All rights reserved.

Name _____ Date _____

"The Geeks Shall Inherit the Earth" by Alexandra Robbins
Take Notes for Research

Take Notes: As you research a **person who was considered unconventional in his or her time, but who went on to make a great contribution to society,** you can use the organizer below to take notes from your sources. At the top, identify the person you have chosen to write about. As necessary, continue your notes on the back of this page, on note cards, or in a word-processing document.

The Person: _____

Main Idea _____	**Main Idea** _____
Quotation or Paraphrase _____	**Quotation or Paraphrase** _____
Source Information _____	**Source Information** _____
Main Idea _____	**Main Idea** _____
Quotation or Paraphrase _____	**Quotation or Paraphrase** _____
Source Information _____	**Source Information** _____

Name _____ Date _____

"The Geeks Shall Inherit the Earth" by Alexandra Robbins
Take Notes for Writing to Sources

Planning Your Argument: Before you begin drafting your **argument**, use the chart below to organize your ideas. In the first box, circle *agree* or *disagree* and then give your reasons.

My Position: I agree/disagree with Robbins's central idea that "Conventional notions of popularity are wrong. What if popularity is not the same thing as social success?"

Here is my analysis of what she means:

_____
_____
_____
_____
_____

Here are details from the text that I will use to evaluate her interpretation of popularity:

_____
_____
_____
_____
_____
_____

Here are details from the text that I will use to support my point of view:

_____
_____
_____
_____
_____

Here is my conclusion: (Summarize your ideas, making clear connections between your analysis of popularity and Robbins's interpretation of popularity.)

_____
_____
_____
_____
_____
_____

Name _____ Date _____

from **Blue Nines and Red Words** by Daniel Tammet
Vocabulary Builder

Selection Vocabulary

    calculating   prime   symmetrical

A. DIRECTIONS: *Write the letter of the word or phrase that best completes each sentence.*

_____ 1. A *prime* number is a number that _____.

    A. can be evenly divided by 10

    B. can be evenly divided by no other number than itself or 1

    C. can be evenly multiplied by no other number than itself or 10

    D. can be evenly multiplied or divided by only the number 2

_____ 2. A person who is busy *calculating* is probably _____.

    A. in the process of writing a math textbook

    B. figuring out the answer to a complicated math problem

    C. assigning various math problems for homework

    D. composing a test for students taking algebra or geometry

_____ 3. A *symmetrical* figure has _____.

    A. equal features on all sides.

    B. a curved top

    C. features that correspond to the metric system

    D. either four or six sides of varying lengths

Academic Vocabulary

    findings   progression   vivid

B. DIRECTIONS: *Write a complete sentence to answer each question. For each item, use a vocabulary word from above in place of the underlined word or words with similar meaning.*

1. What kind of nonfiction book would have very <u>distinct</u> descriptions of events?
_____

2. What <u>results</u> might an art student notice if she mixed yellow dye with blue dye?
_____

3. What <u>series</u> of odd numbers occurs between 1 and 10?
_____

Name _____ Date _____

from Blue Nines and Red Words by Daniel Tammet
Take Notes for Discussion

Before the Group Discussion: Read the following passage from the selection. Then, fill out the chart below with ideas you would like to discuss and examples from the text that illustrate your ideas.

> If I see a number I experience as particularly beautiful on a shop sign or a car license plate, there's a shiver of excitement and pleasure. On the other hand, if the numbers don't match my experience of them—if, for example, a shop sign's price has "99 pence" in red or green (instead of blue)—then I find that uncomfortable and irritating.

Discussion Questions	My Ideas	Examples from the Text
1. How is Tammet's life both similar to and different from that of most people?		
2. Is Tammet's inability to conform a burden, a benefit, both, or neither?		

During the Discussion: As you discuss each question, take notes on how other students' ideas either differ from or build upon your own.

Discussion Questions	Other Ideas Expressed	Comparison to My Own Ideas
1. How is Tammet's life both similar to and different from that of most people?		
2. Is Tammet's inability to conform a burden, a benefit, both, or neither?		

Name _____ Date _____

from **Blue Nines and Red Words** by Daniel Tammet
Take Notes for Research

Take Notes: As you research **what makes a person a prodigy and how being one can affect that person's life,** you can use the organizer below to take notes from your sources. At the top, define the term *prodigy* and list your two examples. Then use the form to collect your information. As necessary, continue your notes on the back of this page, on note cards, or in a word-processing document.

***A prodigy* is** _____.
Examples include: _____.

Main Idea _____	Main Idea _____
Quotation or Paraphrase _____	Quotation or Paraphrase _____
Source Information _____	Source Information _____
Main Idea _____	Main Idea _____
Quotation or Paraphrase _____	Quotation or Paraphrase _____
Source Information _____	Source Information _____

Name _____ Date _____

from **Blue Nines and Red Words** by Daniel Tammet
Take Notes for Writing to Sources

Planning Your Narrative: Before you begin drafting your **autobiographical narrative,** use the chart below to organize your ideas. Follow the directions at the top of each box.

Identify the trait that you wish to write about.

Introduce a related problem or conflict.

List a clear progression of events to include in your narrative. Be sure to use vivid descriptions to let readers "see" the people and events you will include.

Draft a conclusion in which you reflect on your story and make connections between your experience and Daniel Tammet's experience.

All-in-One Workbook

Name _____ Date _____

New Yorker Cartoon
Vocabulary Builder and Writing to Sources

Academic Vocabulary

    depicts   implied   literal

DIRECTIONS: *Complete each sentence with a word, phrase, or clause that contains a context clue for the underlined word.*

1. The sentence *Mr. Jones is tied up right now* contains an idiom. The <u>literal</u> meaning of the idiom is
   _____.

2. The <u>implied</u> meaning of that sentence is
   _____.

3. Picture two illustrations of that sentence—one with its literal meaning, and one with its implied meaning. The first illustration <u>depicts</u> _____.
   The second illustration depicts _____.

Take Notes for Writing to Sources

Planning Your Narrative: Before you begin drafting your **short story,** use the chart below to organize your ideas. Follow the directions at the top of each box.

1. Describe the scene and introduce the main character(s).
2. Introduce the conflict. Tell how, when, and where it happened.
3. Introduce the scene pictured in the cartoon, and use it as the climax of your story. Use vivid details and dialogue to make it come to life.
4. Draft a conclusion to the story. Tell how the conflict is resolved.

Name _____ Date _____

Unit 2: Types of Nonfiction
Big Question Vocabulary—1

The Big Question: Is knowledge the same as understanding?

Most people have had the experience of not fully understanding something. Sometimes this happens even when you have knowledge of facts.

ambiguous: unclear; having more than one meaning

clarify: to make something clearer and easier to understand

comprehend: to understand something that is complicated or difficult

concept: an idea of how something is or how something should be done

information: facts or details about something

DIRECTIONS: Your teachers might as well be speaking a foreign language. You just do not understand! Use all of the vocabulary words to ask your teachers to explain their statements again and in more detail.

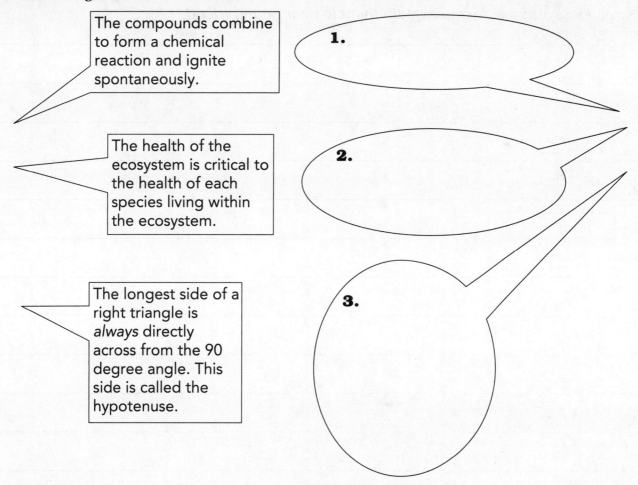

All-in-One Workbook
© Pearson Education, Inc. All rights reserved.

Name _____ Date _____

Unit 2: Types of Nonfiction
Big Question Vocabulary—2

The Big Question: Is knowledge the same as understanding?

Most students have had the experience of gathering data and ideas for a report or project. In the case of a complicated topic, students often must pore over the data they have gathered in order to gain understanding.

fact: a piece of information that is known to be true

interpret: to understand something to have a particular meaning

research: to study or investigate something in detail

sources: people, books, or documents that supply you with information

statistics: a set of numbers that represent facts or measurements

DIRECTIONS: *Write some guidelines for a young friend who is doing his first research project and is unsure how to research his topic. Use all of the vocabulary words in your instructions, and feel free to explain them to your young friend.*

1.

2.

3.

4.

Name _____ Date _____

Unit 2: Types of Nonfiction
Big Question Vocabulary—3

The Big Question: Is knowledge the same as understanding?

One way of getting information is experiencing it for ourselves. The only way to know if you like chocolate is to taste it. Similarly, we should pay attention to feelings, or "vibes," that we get about situations or people.

connection: the process or result of joining two or more things together

feeling: an opinion or a belief about something that is influenced by emotions

insight: clear or deep perception or understanding of something

instinct: the natural ability to think, behave, or react in a particular way without learning it or thinking about it first

sensory: involving one or more of the five senses: taste, touch, hearing, sight, and smell

DIRECTIONS: Write your thoughts in a situation where you had a strong feeling about something but couldn't really explain why. Use all of the vocabulary words.

Name _____ Date _____

Unit 2: Types of Nonfiction
Applying the Big Question

The Big Question: Is knowledge the same as understanding?

DIRECTIONS: Complete the chart below to apply what you have learned about knowledge and understanding. One row has been completed for you.

Example	What facts and information the author had	What knowledge the author gained	What the author came to understand	What I Learned
From Literature	In "On Summer," the author's friend has cancer.	Her friend faced life courageously.	We understand life better when others share their knowledge and experience.	Taking the time to understand others gives life more meaning.
From Literature				
From Science				
From Social Studies				
From Real Life				

Name _____ Date _____

"**On Summer**" by Lorraine Hansberry

Writing About the Big Question

Is knowledge the same as understanding?

Big Question Vocabulary

ambiguous	clarify	comprehend	concept	connection
fact	feeling	information	insight	instinct
interpret	research	senses/sensory	sources	statistics

A. *Use one or more words from the list above to complete each sentence.*

1. To try to understand summer, Hansberry recalls _____ gathered through her _____.

2. Her _____ with the woman in Maine added to her understanding.

3. Observing the woman's pain and laughter gave her the knowledge to partly _____ the meaning of the person's life.

4. However, she knows that a _____ about someone is only useful if we _____ it.

B. *Describe a time when you made a connection with someone. How did this connection help you understand him or her? Write three or four sentences. Use at least two of the Big Question vocabulary words.*

_____
_____
_____
_____

C. *In "On Summer," Lorraine Hansberry's growing understanding of life has changed her feelings about summer. Complete the sentence below. Then, write a short paragraph in which you connect this experience to the Big Question.*

Learning the facts of people's lives may change how we comprehend them because

_____
_____
_____
_____
_____

Name _____ Date _____

"**On Summer**" by Lorraine Hansberry
Literary Analysis: Style

An author's **style** is his or her unique way of writing. Style includes every feature of a writer's use of language. Some elements that contribute to an author's style are

- **Diction:** the kinds of words the author uses
- **Syntax:** the way in which the author arranges words in sentences
- **Tone:** the author's attitude toward his or her audience or subject

A writer's diction and syntax might be described as formal or informal, technical or ordinary, sophisticated or down-to-earth. A writer's tone might be described as serious or playful, friendly or distant, sympathetic or scathing.

DIRECTIONS: Consider the diction and syntax in the italicized passages from "On Summer" in the left-hand column below. Then write notes or a sentence in the right-hand column to describe the tone produced by these features of Hansberry's style.

Passage	Tone
1. The adolescence, admittedly lingering still, brought the traditional passionate commitment to melancholy autumn—*and all that.*	1.
2. By duration alone, for instance, a summer's day seemed *maddeningly excessive, an utter overstatement.*	2.
3. And it was also *cool and sweet* to be on the grass and there was usually the scent of freshly cut lemons or melons in the air.	3.
4. The woman that I met was *as wrinkled as a prune and could hardly hear and barely see and always seemed to be thinking of other times.*	4.
5. I heard later that she did live to see another summer. *And I have retained my respect for the noblest of the seasons.*	5.

Name _____ Date _____

"On Summer" by Lorraine Hansberry
Reading: Generate Prior Questions to Identify Main Idea and Details

The **main idea** is the central message, insight, or opinion in a work of nonfiction. **Supporting details** are the pieces of evidence that a writer uses to prove the main idea. These details can include facts, statistics, quotations, or anecdotes. To **identify the main idea and supporting details** in a work, **generate questions prior to reading.** Before you read, you can ask yourself questions such as

- Why did the author choose this title?
- How might events in the author's life influence his or her attitude toward the subject?

As you read, look for details that answer those questions and point to the main idea.

A. DIRECTIONS: *Answer the following questions to guide your reading of "On Summer."*

1. The word *on*, meaning "concerning" or "about," has been used in the titles of many essays. What expectations does Hansberry's title create in you, the reader?
   _____
   _____

2. In her first sentence, Hansberry declares, "It has taken me a good number of years to come to any measure of respect for summer." What does this opening sentence lead you to expect about the structure of Hansberry's essay?
   _____
   _____

3. A crucial fact about Hansberry's own life was her struggle against cancer and her premature death from the disease at age thirty-four. How do you think this biographical fact might affect the writer's attitude toward the seasons and the passage of time?
   _____
   _____

B. DIRECTIONS: *In an essay about summer, what kind of main idea might you expect? What sorts of supporting details might you find in such an essay? Support your answer with examples from your own experience or from your reading.*

   _____
   _____
   _____
   _____

Name _____ Date _____

"On Summer" by Lorraine Hansberry
Vocabulary Builder

Word List

aloofness   apex   bias   duration   melancholy   pretentious

A. DIRECTIONS: *Revise each sentence so that the underlined vocabulary word is used logically. Be sure not to change the vocabulary word.*

1. Because she mingles easily with her classmates, she has a reputation for aloofness.
   _____

2. The team's unexpected victory created intense feelings of melancholy in the stands.
   _____

3. Thoroughly pretentious, he always dresses casually and simply.
   _____

4. He felt that this failure was surely bound to be the apex of his career.
   _____

5. The chairperson acted with clear bias when she chose the best qualified person.
   _____

6. I knew I was out for the duration of the season when the doctor said my injury was minor.
   _____

B. WORD STUDY: The Latin root *-dur-* means "to harden, hold out, last." Answer each of these questions using one of these words containing the root *-dur-*: endure, durable, duress.

1. Why is a stone sculpture more durable than an ice sculpture?
   _____

2. What might someone with a toothache have to endure?
   _____

3. Why isn't it fair to use duress to get someone to do something for you?
   _____

Name _____ Date _____

"On Summer" by Lorraine Hansberry
Conventions: Direct and Indirect Objects

A **direct object** is the noun or pronoun that receives the action of a verb. You can determine whether a word is a direct object by asking *whom?* or *what?* after an action verb.

    In her essay, Hansberry praises *summer*. [praises *what?*]

    Lorraine admired the old woman. [admired *whom?*]

    An **indirect object** is a noun or pronoun that names the person or thing that receives the action of the verb. You can tell whether a word is the indirect object by finding the direct object and asking *to / for whom?* or *to / for what?* after the action verb. An indirect object always comes between the subject and the direct object, and it never appears in a sentence without a direct object.

    The old woman gave Lorraine courage. [*gave courage to whom?*]

A. DIRECTIONS: *Identify each direct object and indirect object in the sentences below by writing the objects on the line provided. After each object, write* D.O. *for direct object and* I.O. *for indirect object. Note: Some sentences will have both a direct and an indirect object.*

1. In her essay "On Summer," Lorraine Hansberry tells several anecdotes.
   _____

2. Hansberry's observations offer us a subtle portrait of summer.
   _____

3. Clearly, Lorraine Hansberry greatly admired the beautiful hills.
   _____

4. The mother secretly left the runaway boy food.
   _____

B. Writing Application: *On the lines below, write a paragraph in which you compare and contrast Lorraine Hansberry's feelings about summer with your own feelings about that season. Use at least two direct objects and two indirect objects in your writing. Underline each direct object once and each indirect object twice.*

_____
_____
_____
_____
_____
_____
_____
_____

Name _____ Date _____

"On Summer" by Lorraine Hansberry
Support for Writing to Sources: Response to Literature

For your analysis in response to literature, use the chart below to jot down notes under each heading. Include reasons, photos, and quotations to support your purpose.

Order of Events in Hansberry's Life	Details Showing Hansberry's Feelings about Events

Conclusions:
_____
_____
_____
_____

Now, use your notes to write your analysis: Be sure that you analyze how Hansberry's feelings change over time.

Name _____ Date _____

"On Summer" by Lorraine Hansberry
Support for Speaking and Listening: Panel Discussion

Use the chart below to jot down notes for taking part in a panel discussion on how the attitudes and opinions of others do or do not shape our beliefs.

Evidence from the Selection	
Do Shape Our Beliefs	**Do Not Shape Our Beliefs**

Other Evidence	
Do Shape Our Beliefs	**Do Not Shape Our Beliefs**

Name _____ Date _____

"The News" by Neil Postman
Writing About the Big Question

Is knowledge the same as understanding?

Big Question Vocabulary

ambiguous	clarify	comprehend	concept	connection
fact	feeling	information	insight	instinct
interpret	research	senses/sensory	sources	statistics

A. *Use one or more words from the list above to complete each sentence.*

1. Every example and _____ Postman gives about TV news helps us understand how that medium works.

2. If news is _____, it cannot help us understand what is happening.

3. Adam does _____ to gain knowledge and come to an understanding.

4. He wants to gain _____ into how laws are passed.

B. *Follow the directions in responding to each item below.*

1. List three ways that you get news about current events.
   _____
   _____

2. Pick one of the methods you listed above. Tell how the information helps you understand how events in the news affect your personal life. Use at least two of the Big Question vocabulary words.
   _____
   _____

C. *In "The News," the author describes the presentation of television news. Complete the sentence below. Then, write a short paragraph in which you connect this experience to the Big Question.*

We react in different ways to the presentations of news information on television and to the presentations in other media because _____
_____
_____
_____
_____

Name _____ Date _____

"The News" by Neil Postman
Literary Analysis: Expository Essay

An **expository essay** is a short piece of nonfiction that presents information, discusses ideas, or explains a process. In a good expository essay, the writer provides evidence and examples to present an accurate and complete view of the topic. The writer may also use one or more of the following techniques to provide support, depth, and context.

- **Description:** including language that appeals to the senses
- **Comparison and contrast:** showing similarities and differences among two or more items
- **Cause and effect:** explaining the relationship between events, actions, or situations by showing how one can result in another

DIRECTIONS: *Use the lines provided to answer the questions about Neil Postman's expository essay.*

1. What is the topic that Postman discusses in his essay "The News"?
   _____

2. In paragraphs 7–10, Postman discusses the "structure" of a typical television newscast. Give three specific details that Postman includes in his description of a typical television newscast.
   _____
   _____
   _____

3. How does this description relate to Postman's main idea in the essay?
   _____
   _____

4. Postman compares and contrasts TV news and print media (newspapers and magazines). Briefly summarize three ways in which they are alike or different.
   _____
   _____
   _____
   _____
   _____

5. How does this comparison and contrast support the writer's main idea in the essay?
   _____
   _____

6. According to Postman, what underlying cause explains the fact that the national evening news has not expanded from a half-hour format to a full hour?
   _____
   _____

Name _____ Date _____

"The News" by Neil Postman
Reading: Reread to Identify Main Idea and Details

The **main idea** is the central message, insight, or opinion in a work of nonfiction. The **supporting details** in a work help to prove the writer's point. These details can include facts, statistics, quotations, or anecdotes. To help you **identify the main idea and supporting details** in a work, **reread** passages that do not seem to support the work's main idea.

- As you read, note key details to form ideas about what the main idea might be.
- If a detail does not seem to support that main idea, reread the passage to be sure you have not misinterpreted it.
- If necessary, revise your assumptions about the main idea.

DIRECTIONS: *Answer the following questions to guide your reading of "The News."*

1. Reread paragraphs three and four of the essay. Why does Postman describe moving pictures of a burning aircraft carrier as "interesting" and pictures of toppling buildings as "exciting"?

   _____
   _____
   _____

2. According to Postman, why do visual changes on TV have to be more dramatic to be interesting? (Reread the paragraph beginning, "The television screen is smaller than life.")

   _____
   _____
   _____

3. What does Postman mean when he connects television news broadcasts to the "realm of the symbolic"? (Reread the seventh and eighth paragraphs of the essay.)

   _____
   _____
   _____

4. How does the author support his claim that "it is the trivial event that is often best suited for television coverage"? (Reread the long paragraph that begins, "While the form of a news broadcast emphasizes tidiness and control. . . .")

   _____
   _____
   _____

All-in-One Workbook
© Pearson Education, Inc. All rights reserved.

Name _____   Date _____

"The News" by Neil Postman
Vocabulary Builder

Word List

> compensation   daunting   imposition   medium   revered   temporal

A. DIRECTIONS: *Revise each sentence so that the underlined vocabulary word is used logically. Be sure not to change the vocabulary word.*

1. She settled her lawsuit for a substantial amount, refusing all <u>compensation</u> for her injuries.
   _____

2. The climb to the summit seemed <u>daunting</u>, and we thought it would be an easy hike.
   _____

3. Ana pays attention to the <u>temporal</u> realities of her job and is almost always late to work.
   _____

4. "It is because you are a <u>revered</u> expert," she said, "that we feel free to disregard your opinion."
   _____

5. A newspaper is a type of <u>medium</u> in which it is rare to find interviews.
   _____

6. The <u>imposition</u> of a rule against leaving early gave students greater freedom.
   _____

B. WORD STUDY: The Latin root *-temp-* means "time." Answer each of these questions using one of these words containing the root *-temp-*: *temporary* (for a short time), *temporize* (to do something to gain time), *contemporary* (at the current time).

1. Why isn't President Washington a <u>contemporary</u> president?
   _____

2. When can you tell that a situation is not <u>temporary</u>?
   _____

3. Why would someone <u>temporize</u> if he were caught doing something wrong?
   _____

Name _____ Date _____

"The News" by Neil Postman
Conventions: Predicate Nominatives and Predicate Adjectives

A **predicate nominative** is a noun or pronoun that appears with a linking verb. (Linking verbs include *become, grow, look, seem,* and all forms of *be.*) A predicate nominative renames, identifies, or explains the subject of the sentence. In a sentence with a predicate nominative, the linking verb acts as an equal sign between the subject and the predicate nominative. They refer to the same person or thing. In the following examples, the subject is in boldface, the linking verb is in italics, and the predicate nominative is underlined.

My **brother** *was* a media critic.

This *is* the problem with television news.

A **predicate adjective** is an adjective that appears with a linking verb and describes the subject of the sentence. In the following examples, the subject is in bold type, the linking verb is in italics, and the predicate adjective is underlined.

The **aircraft carrier** *seemed* enormous.

Through the pollutant haze, some **colors** *looked* muted.

A. DIRECTIONS: *In each of the following sentences, circle the linking verb. Then, underline each predicate nominative once and each predicate adjective twice.*

1. The television screen is smaller than life.
2. In the cinema, the situation is somewhat different.
3. But they are also symbols of a dominant theme of television news.
4. Another severe limitation on television is time.
5. Watching television becomes an obsession for some people.
6. Television news is a source of entertainment for many people.
7. During a power outage, night television is useless for getting news about the weather.
8. Television news seems very profitable for the broadcast stations.

B. Writing Application: *On the lines below, write a paragraph in which you describe your favorite television show. In your paragraph, use at least two predicate nominatives and two predicate adjectives. Underline each predicate nominative once and each predicate adjective twice.*

_____
_____
_____
_____
_____
_____

Name _____ Date _____

"The News" by Neil Postman
Support for Writing to Sources: Explanatory Essay

For your explanatory essay, use the lines below to jot down notes under each heading.

News Source: _____

PROS	CONS

How Neil Postman might feel about the twenty-first century source:
_____
_____
_____

Conclusion:
_____
_____
_____

Now, use your notes to write your explanatory essay.

Name _____ Date _____

"The News" by Neil Postman
Support for Research and Technology: Journal Entries

Tell how two different forms of media provide information about a subject of great news coverage. Use the lines below to make notes for your journal entry.

Subject (Figure in the News):	
Source of News Story A:	**Source of News Story B:**

Questions	Answers and Details
Do the stories agree about facts? Do the stories emphasize different aspects of the subject's life?	

Summary of Findings:

Name _____ Date _____

"**Libraries Face Sad Chapter**" by Pete Hamill
Writing About the Big Question

Is knowledge the same as understanding?

Big Question Vocabulary

ambiguous	clarify	comprehend	concept	connection
fact	feeling	information	insight	instinct
interpret	research	senses/sensory	sources	statistics

A. *Use one or more words from the list above to complete each sentence.*

1. _____ alone only tell us facts; they do not help us understand.

2. Libraries are _____ of _____ that lead us toward knowledge and understanding.

3. John went to the library to do _____ on the Carnegie libraries.

4. He wanted to gain _____ into Carnegie's motive for donating so much money.

B. *Follow the directions in responding to each item below.*

1. Describe two recent occasions when you used the library to do research.
   _____
   _____

2. How could you make better use of your time in the library? Give one example. Use at least two of the Big Question vocabulary words.
   _____
   _____

C. *In "Libraries Face Sad Chapter," the author urges readers to contribute to a fund to support public libraries, a source of knowledge. Complete the sentence below. Then, write a short paragraph in which you connect this experience to the Big Question.*

Libraries, as a source of information and a place for research, are still important because _____
_____
_____
_____
_____
_____
_____

All-in-One Workbook
© Pearson Education, Inc. All rights reserved.

Name _____ Date _____

"Libraries Face Sad Chapter" by Pete Hamill
Literary Analysis: Persuasive Essay

A **persuasive essay** is a short nonfiction work that tries to persuade a reader to think or act in a particular way. Persuasive essays usually include one or both of the following:

- **Appeals to reason:** logical arguments based on verifiable evidence, such as facts, statistics, or expert testimony
- **Appeals to emotion:** statements intended to affect listeners' feelings about a subject. These statements often include charged language—words with strong positive or negative associations.

DIRECTIONS: *Answer these questions about Pete Hamill's persuasive essay.*

1. What is Pete Hamill's opinion and suggested course of action in his essay "Libraries Face Sad Chapter"? State the writer's position in your own words.
   _____
   _____

2. Identify two logical arguments Hamill uses to support his case for the importance of libraries and freely circulating books.
   _____
   _____
   _____
   _____

3. Reread the following excerpt from the essay:

   No teacher sent us to those leathery cliffs of books. Reading wasn't an assignment; it was a pleasure. We read for the combined thrills of villainy and heroism, along with the knowledge of the vast world beyond the parish. Living in those other worlds, we could become other people

   In this passage, what are two words or phrases with strong emotional associations? Are these emotional associations positive or negative? Explain your answer.
   _____
   _____
   _____
   _____

4. At the end of his essay on libraries, Hamill stresses a "debt" that must be honored. On the lines below, explain how Hamill conceives of this "debt" and why it does (or does not) constitute an effective conclusion for his persuasive essay.
   _____
   _____
   _____
   _____

"Libraries Face Sad Chapter" by Pete Hamill
Reading: Reread to Analyze and Evaluate Persuasive Appeals

Persuasive appeals in an essay are the arguments the author makes to persuade readers or listeners to think or act in a particular way. To **analyze and evaluate persuasive appeals,** identify passages in which the author makes an argument in support of his or her position. Then, **reread** those passages to test the logic and reasoning of the author's arguments. Ask yourself these questions:

- Is the author's argument supported by evidence, or is it based on faulty assumptions?
- Does the author demonstrate clear connections between ideas, or does the author make leaps in logic?

A. DIRECTIONS: *Answer the following questions about Pete Hamill's use of persuasive appeals in "Libraries Face Sad Chapter."*

1. Reread the first section of the essay. Why do you think Hamill chose to open this essay with a reminiscence of how he and his friends used libraries in their childhood?

_____
_____
_____
_____

2. According to Hamill, why are libraries more important than ever in hard times? In the section "Built by Carnegie," what arguments does Hamill use to support this opinion?

_____
_____
_____
_____

3. Reread the section entitled "Immigrants' Appreciation." In your opinion, does Hamill appeal primarily to reason or to emotion in this section? Use specific references to the text to explain your answer.

_____
_____
_____
_____

B. DIRECTIONS: *On the lines below, explain how Hamill uses a mixture of idealism and realism to appeal to his audience. Is this combination effective, in your opinion? Why or why not?*

_____
_____
_____
_____

Name _____ Date _____

"Libraries Face Sad Chapter" by Pete Hamill
Vocabulary Builder

Word List

curtailed   duration   emulate   medium   presumed   volumes

A. DIRECTIONS: Revise each sentence so that the underlined vocabulary word is used logically. Be sure not to change the vocabulary word.

1. We were pleased to find out that the duration of the restaurant wait time was longer than half an hour.

2. The championship tennis match was curtailed by rain, leaving the spectators certain about the outcome.

3. Since e-mail is a rapid and cheap medium, its popularity today is hard to explain.

4. If the author wrote so many books, why are so many volumes of his work in the library?

5. We presumed that she was going with us, so we did not wait for her.

6. Alexandra likes to emulate her sister, so she never wears the same kind of clothes.

B. WORD STUDY: The Latin root -sum- means "to take." Answer each of the following questions using one of these words containing -sum-: consumer, assumption, and resume.

1. How does a consumer usually get what he or she wants?

2. What happened as a result of Columbus's assumption that the world is round?

3. When do TV programs resume when commercials interrupt the broadcast?

All-in-One Workbook
© Pearson Education, Inc. All rights reserved.

Name _____ Date _____

"Libraries Face Sad Chapter" by Pete Hamill
Conventions: Colons, Semicolons, and Ellipsis Points

Use a **colon** in order to introduce a list of items following an independent clause, to introduce a formal quotation, or to follow the salutation in a business letter.

- He bought ingredients for the salad: lettuce, tomatoes, onions, and radishes.
- The reason for cutting services, hours, and staff at libraries is the same: money, or the lack of it.
- Dear Sir:

Use a **semicolon** to join related independent clauses that are not already joined by a coordinating conjunction. Also, use a semicolon to avoid confusion when independent clauses or items in a series already contain commas.

- Hamill claims that as a schoolboy, reading wasn't an assignment; it was a pleasure.
- We visited Boston, Philadelphia, and Washington, D.C.; altogether, our tour of the eastern seaboard was a great success.

Ellipsis points (. . .) are punctuation marks that are used to show that something has not been expressed. Usually, ellipsis points indicate one of the following situations:
Words have been left out of a quotation.
A series continues beyond the items mentioned.
Time passes or action occurs in a narrative.

- Pete Hamill says that "When I was a boy, the rooms were crowded with immigrants . . . with people who came from places where there were no libraries for the poor."
- We thought wistfully about the cats' curiosity, agility, and grace. . . .
- They keep their discontent to themselves . . . but will they do so forever?

A. Directions: *Rewrite each sentence on the lines provided, correcting errors in the use of colons, semicolons, and ellipsis points. There is only one error in each sentence.*

1. Julius Caesar described his victory as follows . . . "I came, I saw, I conquered."
   _____

2. Public libraries are a rare gift, generations of immigrants, adults and children included, have risen out of poverty and ignorance because of them.
   _____
   _____

B. Writing Application: *On the lines, write a paragraph in which you describe a favorite animal or bird. In your paragraph, use at least one example of each of the following: a colon, a semicolon, and ellipsis points.*

_____
_____
_____
_____
_____

All-in-One Workbook

Name _____ Date _____

"Libraries Face Sad Chapter" by Pete Hamill
Support for Writing to Sources: Informative Text (Abstract)

For your abstract, use the chart below to jot down notes under each heading.

Topic: _____
_____

Main Idea: _____
_____

Supporting Details:

1. _____
_____
_____

2. _____
_____
_____

3. _____
_____
_____

4. _____
_____
_____

Now, use your notes to write your abstract. Give enough information so that someone who has not yet read the essay can get a clear understanding of what the essay is about.

Name _____ Date _____

"Libraries Face Sad Chapter" by Pete Hamill
Support for Research and Technology:
Build and Present Knowledge

To prepare for your persuasive speech, use the chart below to gather information for a **comparative chart** that will show the library services offered and the average numbers of people using them.

LIBRARY SERVICES	AVERAGE NUMBER OF PEOPLE USING SERVICE
1.	
2.	
3.	
4.	

SOURCES:
_____
_____
_____

SUMMARIZING STATEMENT:
_____
_____
_____
_____
_____

Name _____ Date _____

"I Have a Dream" by Martin Luther King, Jr.
Writing About the Big Question

Is knowledge the same as understanding?

Big Question Vocabulary

ambiguous	clarify	comprehend	concept	connection
fact	feeling	information	insight	instinct
interpret	research	senses/sensory	sources	statistics

A. *Use one or more words from the list above to complete each sentence.*

1. The _____ helped Jill understand the civil rights movement.

2. King spoke with great _____ that helped people understand his message.

3. He made a powerful _____ with his audience as he gave them information on the injustices suffered by many people.

4. Andrew better understood King's appeal when he read _____ about all the people who went to hear King speak.

B. *Follow the directions in responding to each item below.*

1. When have you heard a good speaker? Describe the occasion.
   _____
   _____

2. How did the speaker help you understand the topic? What techniques or methods did the speaker use? Use at least two of the Big Question vocabulary words.
   _____
   _____

C. In "I Have a Dream," Martin Luther King makes a logical and emotional speech to help listeners understand his dream of freedom and equality. Complete the sentence below. Then, write a short paragraph in which you connect this experience to the Big Question.

The concept of equality might be ambiguous to some people because _____
_____
_____
_____
_____

All-in-One Workbook
© Pearson Education, Inc. All rights reserved.

Name _____ Date _____

"I Have a Dream" by Martin Luther King, Jr.
Literary Analysis: Persuasive Speech

A **persuasive speech** is a speech that tries to convince listeners to think or act in a certain way. Persuasive speeches may appeal to reason or emotion or both. In order to engage the audience, speakers often include **rhetorical devices,** special patterns of words and ideas that create emphasis and stir emotion in the audience. Common rhetorical devices include the following:

- **Parallelism:** repeating a grammatical structure or arrangement of words to create a sense of rhythm and momentum
- **Restatement:** expressing the same idea in different words to clarify and stress key points
- **Repetition:** expressing different ideas using the same words or images in order to reinforce concepts and unify the speech

DIRECTIONS: *Read each of the following passages from King's "I Have a Dream" speech. On the lines provided, identify the rhetorical device or devices in each passage. (You may find more than one rhetorical device.) Then briefly explain your answer by citing the words and phrases that exemplify the device.*

1. But one hundred years later, the Negro still is not free. One hundred years later, the life of the Negro is still sadly crippled by the manacles of segregation and the chains of discrimination. One hundred years later, the Negro lives on a lonely island of poverty in the midst of a vast ocean of material prosperity.

    Rhetorical Device(s): _____

    Explanation: _____
    _____
    _____

2. When the architects of our republic wrote the magnificent words of the Constitution and the Declaration of Independence, they were signing a promissory note to which every American was to fall heir. This note was a promise that all men . . . would be guaranteed the unalienable rights of life, liberty, and the pursuit of happiness.

    Rhetorical Device(s): _____

    Explanation: _____
    _____
    _____

3. It is obvious today that America has defaulted on this promissory note insofar as her citizens of color are concerned. Instead of honoring this sacred obligation, America has given the Negro people a bad check; a check which has come back marked "insufficient funds."

    Rhetorical Device(s): _____

    Explanation: _____
    _____
    _____

Name _____ Date _____

"I Have a Dream" by Martin Luther King, Jr.
Reading: Evaluate Persuasion

Persuasive techniques are devices used to influence the audience in favor of the author's argument. In addition to presenting evidence in a persuasive speech, a speaker may use the following:

- emotionally charged language
- rhetorical devices, such as parallelism, restatement, and repetition

To analyze and evaluate persuasive techniques, **read aloud** to hear the effect. Notice the emotional impact of the sounds of certain words, as well as the rhythm and momentum created by the word patterns that the author uses. Consider both the purpose and effect of these persuasive techniques and evaluate the author's success in using them to make a convincing argument.

DIRECTIONS: *Read the following excerpts from "I Have a Dream." Then, on the lines provided, answer the questions that follow.*

1. Five score years ago, a great American, in whose symbolic shadow we stand today, signed the Emancipation Proclamation.

   A. To which "great American" does King allude in this sentence? _____

   B. What place does King refer to in saying "in whose symbolic shadow we stand"? _____

   C. What well-known speech in American history does King echo in saying "five score years ago"? _____

2. Now is the time to make real the promises of Democracy.
   Now is the time to rise from the dark and desolate valley of segregation to the sunlit path of racial justice.

   A. How does this passage illustrate parallelism? _____
   _____

   B. What emotionally charged words or phrases does King use in this passage? _____
   _____

3. This sweltering summer of the Negro's legitimate discontent will not pass until there is an invigorating autumn of freedom and equality.

   A. What image dominates this passage? _____
   _____

   B. How does the passage illustrate parallelism? _____
   _____

Name _____ Date _____

"I Have a Dream" by Dr. Martin Luther King, Jr.
Vocabulary Builder

Word List

creed   defaulted   degenerate   hallowed   momentous   oppression

A. DIRECTIONS: *In each item, think about the meaning of the underlined word and then answer the question.*

1. If you think that a certain place is hallowed ground, would you consider it with respect or indifference? Explain.
   _____

2. If the condition of your house were to degenerate over the next few years, what might you do?
   _____

3. Why do people often take photographs during momentous occasions in their lives?
   _____

4. How would you feel if you loaned a friend some money and he defaulted on his promise to pay it back?
   _____

5. Why do you think many people dislike living under oppression?
   _____

6. Do you think most people take a creed seriously? Why or why not?
   _____

B. WORD STUDY: The Latin root *-cred-* means "to trust, to believe." Answer each of the following questions using one of these words containing *-cred-*: *credence* ("the act of believing"), *credible* ("believable"), *credulous* ("ready to believe").

1. Why isn't it wise to give credence to everything you hear on commercials?
   _____

2. Why do lawyers want credible witnesses to support their case?
   _____

3. What kind of trouble might someone who is too credulous get into?
   _____

Name _____ Date _____

"I Have a Dream" by Martin Luther King, Jr.
Conventions: Independent and Dependent Clauses

A **clause** is a group of words that contains a subject and a verb. An **independent clause** is a complete sentence. A **dependent clause** has a subject and a verb but is not a complete thought. Dependent clauses can function as noun, adjective, or adverbial clauses.

Adverbial clauses begin with subordinating conjunctions such as *when, though, if, after,* and *because.* Adjective clauses begin with relative pronouns such as *who, which, whose,* and *that.* Pronouns such as *whatever, whoever, whomever,* and *however* often begin noun clauses. In these examples, the independent clause is underlined and the dependent clause is italicized.

Independent Clause:	"I Have a Dream" is Martin Luther King, Jr.'s most well-known speech.
Independent Clause, Dependent Clause:	Martin Luther King, Jr., was a leader *who inspired millions of people.*
Dependent Clause, Independent Clause:	*When King was awarded the Nobel Peace Prize,* people cheered.

A. PRACTICE: *Rewrite each independent clause as a sentence. If the item is a dependent clause, add an independent clause to it to form a complete sentence.*

1. when King repeated, "Let freedom ring,"
   _____

2. after King ended his speech
   _____

3. King spoke with fervor
   _____

4. he sought justice
   _____

B. Writing Application: *Combine each of the following pairs of sentences into one sentence by using a subordinating conjunction or relative pronoun to change one independent clause into a dependent clause.*

1. African Americans could not stay in hotels. They did not have equality.
   _____

2. King began speaking. Everyone listened.
   _____

3. King spoke to the people. The people vowed to have faith in justice.
   _____

Name _____ Date _____

"I Have a Dream" by Dr. Martin Luther King, Jr.
Support for Writing to Sources: Proposal

Use the lines below to make prewriting notes for your proposal.

1. **Reasons "I Have a Dream Day" should be celebrated:** _____
   _____
   _____
   _____

2. **Official or agency to address:** _____
   _____
   _____
   _____

3. **Evidence or examples from King's speech to develop argument:** _____
   _____
   _____
   _____

4. **Possible counterarguments:** _____
   _____
   _____
   _____

5. **Response to counterarguments:** _____
   _____
   _____
   _____

Now use your notes to write your proposal.

Name _____ Date _____

"I Have a Dream" by Dr. Martin Luther King, Jr.
Support for Speaking and Listening: Radio News Report

Use the following lines to make prewriting notes for your radio news report and commentary.

Background Information: _____
_____
_____
_____
_____
_____
_____
_____

Notable Excerpts From the Speech: _____
_____
_____
_____
_____
_____
_____
_____

Effect of the Speech on the Crowd: _____
_____
_____
_____
_____
_____
_____
_____

Name _____ Date _____

from **Silent Spring** by Rachel Carson
"If I Forget Thee, Oh Earth . . ." by Arthur C. Clarke

Writing About the Big Question

Is knowledge the same as understanding?

Big Question Vocabulary

ambiguous	clarify	comprehend	concept	connection
fact	feeling	information	insight	instinct
interpret	research	senses/sensory	sources	statistics

A. *Use one or more words from the list above to complete each sentence.*

1. Marvin's father had a deep _____ to Earth.

2. In his story, Clarke tries to give his readers _____ into the preciousness of Earth.

3. Rachel Carson uses a fictional setting to help readers _____ what could happen with the continued use of pesticides.

4. Carson uses _____ images to help readers visualize the silent spring.

B. *Follow the directions in responding to each item below.*

1. List two facts you know about the environment.
   _____
   _____

2. Write two sentences telling how the facts you listed above help you understand the importance of caring for the environment. Use at least two of the Big Question vocabulary words.
   _____
   _____

C. *Both Clarke and Carson, in different ways, explain what can happen if we destroy our environment. Complete the sentence below. Then, write a short paragraph in which you connect this experience to the Big Question.*

Knowing how fragile the environment can be can give insight into
_____
_____
_____

Name _____ Date _____

"If I Forget Thee, Oh Earth . . ." by Arthur C. Clarke
from Silent Spring by Rachel Carson
Literary Analysis: Theme

The **theme** of a literary work is the central message or insight about life that is conveyed through the work. Sometimes, the theme is stated directly. More often, it is suggested indirectly through the words and experiences of the characters or through the events of a story.

How the theme is developed depends in part on the genre, or form, of the work. In informational text and most other nonfiction, the theme is usually stated directly as the central idea. Then, the writer supports the idea with facts, details, and examples to prove the point.

In fiction, poetry, and plays, the theme is most often implied, or suggested. Readers must figure out the theme by making inferences from characters' behavior, conflicts and resolutions, word choice, symbols, and other details.

DIRECTIONS: Read the following passages, and describe how each passage relates to the selection's theme.

from "If I Forget Thee, Oh Earth . . ."

He was looking upon the funeral pyre of a world—upon the radioactive aftermath of Armageddon. Across a quarter of a million miles of space, the glow of dying atoms was still visible, a perennial reminder of the ruinous past. It would be centuries yet before that deadly glow died from the rocks and life could return again to fill that silent, empty world.

1. What does this passage imply about what has happened to Earth?
   _____

2. How does this passage relate to the theme of the story?
   _____

3. How would you state the theme of this story?
   _____

from Silent Spring

In the gutters under the eaves and between the shingles of the roofs, a white granular powder still showed a few patches; some weeks before it had fallen like snow upon the roofs and lawns, the fields and streams.

No witchcraft, no enemy action had silenced the rebirth of new life in this stricken world. The people had done it themselves.

1. What might the "white granular powder" be? What are the effects of the powder?
   _____

2. How does this passage relate to the theme of the selection?
   _____

3. How would you state the theme of this selection?
   _____

Name _____ Date _____

"If I Forget Thee, Oh Earth . . ." by Arthur C. Clarke
from Silent Spring by Rachel Carson
Vocabulary Builder

Word List

> blight   maladies   moribund   perennial   purged

A. DIRECTIONS: *Revise each sentence so that the underlined vocabulary word is used logically. Be sure not to change the vocabulary word.*

1. I purged the wound on my foot, thereby increasing the chances of infection.
   _____

2. Those flowers are perennials, so you will need to plant them again next year.
   _____

3. Because of the blight, the potatoes we grew were especially fine this year.
   _____

4. Due to various maladies, they became more vigorous and cheerful.
   _____

5. The fact that her garden was moribund filled her with delight.
   _____

B. DIRECTIONS: *Write the letter of the word or phrase that is the best synonym for the Word List word.*

___ 1. perennial
   A. occasional
   B. temporary
   C. perpetual
   D. unusual

___ 2. maladies
   A. complaints
   B. diseases
   C. mistakes
   D. theories

___ 3. moribund
   A. depressing
   B. upsetting
   C. cheering
   D. dying

___ 4. purged
   A. cleansed
   B. destroyed
   C. manufactured
   D. created

Name _____ Date _____

"If I Forget Thee, Oh Earth . . ." by Arthur C. Clarke
from Silent Spring by Rachel Carson
Support for Writing to Sources: Explanatory Text

Use a chart like the one below to make prewriting notes for your essay of comparison and contrast. Then, answer the two questions following the chart.

Points of Comparison/Contrast	"If I Forget Thee . . ."	from Silent Spring
My response to each selection		
Statement of each selection's theme		
Possible reasons why author chose genre		

1. In general, do you think fiction or nonfiction is more effective in expressing a theme? Explain.
   _____
   _____
   _____

2. Which of these two selections do you think is more effective in expressing its theme? Explain.
   _____
   _____
   _____

Name _____ Date _____

Writing Process
Cause-and-Effect Essay

Prewriting: Gathering Details

Use the following graphic organizer to decide whether to explore the causes that produced a central event or the effects the event produced. List the causes and effects and note the key details related to each.

Cause: Key details:	Cause: Key details:

⬇ ⬇

Central Event:

⬇ ⬇

Effect: Key details:	Effect: Key details:

Drafting: Using the TRI Method

Use the chart to help you develop the paragraphs of your essay. To do this, follow the steps listed in the first column for each of your body paragraphs.

TRI Method	Paragraph 1	Paragraph 2	Paragraph 3
Topic:			
Restate your topic.			
Illustrate your point through details, facts, examples, and personal experiences.			

All-in-One Workbook
© Pearson Education, Inc. All rights reserved.

Name _____ Date _____

Writer's Toolbox
Conventions: Subject-Verb Agreement

A verb must agree with its subject in number. A compound subject joined by *and* is plural in number and requires a plural verb.

Plural Subject and Verb: A *salad* and a baked *potato come* with the dinner.

Compound subjects joined by *or* and *nor* are considered singular unless the *last* part is plural.

Singular Subject and Verb: Either two *vegetables* or a <u>salad comes</u> with the dinner.
Plural Subject and Verb: Either a *salad* or two <u>vegetables come</u> with the dinner.

Some indefinite pronouns, such as *each, anyone,* and *everybody,* are always singular. Others, such as *both* and *many,* are always plural.

Singular Subject and Verb: <u>Each</u> of the dinners <u>comes</u> with a salad.
Plural Subject and Verb: <u>Both</u> of the dinners <u>come</u> with a salad.

A few indefinite pronouns, such as *all, none,* and *most,* may be singular or plural, depending on the nouns to which they refer.

Singular Subject and Verb: <u>Most</u> of the <u>food comes</u> with no extra charge.
Plural Subject and Verb: <u>Most</u> of the <u>desserts come</u> with the meal.

Identifying Correct Subject-Verb Agreement

A. DIRECTIONS: *Complete each sentence by underlining the verb in parentheses that agrees with the subject.*

1. A pine and a willow (grows, grow) at the park entrance.
2. Most of the park's trees (thrives, thrive) in the cool climate.
3. Either two oaks or a maple (borders, border) the pond.
4. Most of the park (feels, feel) cool in summer.

Fixing Incorrect Subject-Verb Agreement

B. DIRECTIONS: *On the lines provided, rewrite these sentences so that the subject and verb agree.*

1. Funds for the school system tops the list of town expenses.

2. The library and the civic center costs the town little money.

3. Either fees or a special tax fund the local library.

4. Each of the town board members know the details about the budget.

Name _____ Date _____

"First Inaugural Address" by Franklin Delano Roosevelt
Vocabulary Builder

Selection Vocabulary

arduous   candor   feasible

A. DIRECTIONS: *Revise each sentence so that the underlined vocabulary word is used logically. Be sure not to change the vocabulary word.*

1. Because she always spoke with candor, no one ever believed her.
   _____

2. It is quite feasible that young players who develop their skills will never do well as athletes.
   _____
   _____

3. Because the task was arduous, the workers completed it with little effort.
   _____
   _____

Academic Vocabulary

trace   signaled   accentuate

B. DIRECTIONS: *Write a response to each question. Make sure to use the word in italics at least once in your response.*

1. What would be an effective way to *trace* the important events in Roosevelt's life?
   _____
   _____

2. In an adventure film, the hero's arrival might be *signaled* by what kind of music?
   _____
   _____

3. What punctuation mark is most commonly used to *accentuate* the urgency of a statement?
   _____
   _____

Name _____ Date _____

"First Inaugural Address" by Franklin Delano Roosevelt
Take Notes for Discussion

Before the Debate: Read the following passage from the selection.

> But in the event that the Congress shall fail to take one of these two courses, and in the event that the national emergency is still critical, I shall not evade the clear course of duty that will then confront me.
>
> I shall ask the Congress for the one remaining instrument to meet the crisis—broad executive power to wage a war against the emergency as great as the power that would be given me if we were in fact invaded by a foreign foe.

During the Debate: As you present your views and listen to those of other students, take notes on how their ideas either differ from or build upon your own.

Discussion Questions	Other Ideas Expressed	Comparison to My Own Ideas
1. What is Roosevelt's tone in this passage?		
2. What image of a leader does Roosevelt project in this passage?		
3. Do you think listeners at the time found the message of a "war" on the emergency to be comforting or disturbing?		

All-in-One Workbook
© Pearson Education, Inc. All rights reserved.

Name _____ Date _____

"First Inaugural Address" by Franklin Delano Roosevelt
Take Notes for Writing to Sources

Planning Your Argument: Before you begin drafting your **persuasive essay,** use the chart below to organize your ideas. In the first column, write examples of Roosevelt's charged language. In the second column, **analyze.** Tell what you think he hoped to accomplish by using that particular language. Then, in the third column, **evaluate.** Jot down your opinions regarding whether or not you think the language was effective and appropriate. Support your opinions with reasons.

Examples of Loaded Language	How Roosevelt Hoped to Stir Listeners' Emotions	My Thoughts: Was the Language Effective? Why or Why Not?

Name _____ Date _____

"First Inaugural Address" by Franklin Delano Roosevelt
Take Notes for Research

As you research **the role that the banking industry played in causing the Great Depression,** you can use the organizer below to take notes from your sources. As necessary, continue your notes on the back of this page, on note cards, or in a word-processing document.

The Role the Banking Industry Played in Causing the Great Depression

Main Idea _____

Quotation or Paraphrase _____

Source Information _____

Main Idea _____

Quotation or Paraphrase _____

Source Information _____

Main Idea _____

Quotation or Paraphrase _____

Source Information _____

Main Idea _____

Quotation or Paraphrase _____

Source Information _____

All-in-One Workbook
© Pearson Education, Inc. All rights reserved.

Name _____ Date _____

from Nothing to Fear: Lessons in Leadership from FDR, by Alan Axelrod
Vocabulary Builder

Selection Vocabulary

inevitable   obscures   provocative

A. DIRECTIONS: *Write the letter of the word or phrase that is the best synonym for the italicized word.*

_____ 1. *obscures*

    A. surprises   C. proves to be true

    B. hides from view   D. demands

_____ 2. *provocative*

    A. without fear   C. disappointing

    B. exactly as planned   D. stimulating

_____ 3. *inevitable*

    A. certain to happen   C. unearned

    B. without value   D. surprising or unexpected

Academic Vocabulary

asserts   critique   visionary

B. DIRECTIONS: *Revise each sentence so that the underlined vocabulary word is used logically. Be sure not to change the vocabulary word.*

1. She was a <u>visionary</u> leader who seemed to have no definite plan or purpose in mind.
   _____

2. If she <u>asserts</u> her opinion again, please urge her to express it more strongly.
   _____

3. To give a knowledgeable <u>critique</u> of a book, it is helpful not to have read the author's other works.
   _____

Name _____ Date _____

from Nothing to Fear: Lessons in Leadership from FDR, by Alan Axelrod
Take Notes for Discussion

Before the Group Discussion: Read the following passage from the selection. Then, fill out the chart below with ideas you would like to discuss and examples from the text that support your ideas.

> He didn't ask them to stop being afraid, but to stop letting fear obscure their vision of reality. He asked the people to confront what they feared, so that they could see clearly what needed to be done and thereby overcome (and the word is significant) the terror that paralyzes.

During the Discussion: As you present your views and listen to those of other students, take notes on how their ideas either differ from or build upon your own.

Discussion Questions	Other Ideas Expressed	Comparison to My Own Ideas
1. What does Axelrod find remarkable about FDR's leadership?		
2. The steps Axelrod describes do not involve changes in policy or law, but in attitude. Would such attitude adjustments be important in a time of national crisis like the Great Depression?		

All-in-One Workbook
© Pearson Education, Inc. All rights reserved.

Name _____ Date _____

from Nothing to Fear: Lessons in Leadership from FDR, by Alan Axelrod
Take Notes for Research

As you research **the steps that President Roosevelt took to address the causes and the suffering of the Great Depression** and plan your research report, you can use the organizer below to take notes from your sources. As necessary, continue your notes on the back of this page, on note cards, or in a word-processing document.

Steps taken by FDR to address the sources and relieve the suffering of the Great Depression	
Main Idea _____ **Quotation or Paraphrase** _____ **Source Information** _____ 	**Main Idea** _____ **Quotation or Paraphrase** _____ **Source Information** _____
Main Idea _____ **Quotation or Paraphrase** _____ **Source Information** _____ 	**Main Idea** _____ **Quotation or Paraphrase** _____ **Source Information** _____

Name _____ Date _____

from **Nothing to Fear: Lessons in Leadership from FDR, by** Alan Axelrod
Take Notes for Writing to Sources

Planning Your Argument: Before you begin drafting your **argumentative essay,** use the chart below to organize your ideas. In the first column, write examples of Axelrod's claims regarding President Roosevelt's speech and vision. In the second column, note the evidence Axelrod uses as support. Then, in the third column, **evaluate.** Jot down your opinions regarding whether or not you think the evidence is relevant and sufficient to support his claim. Support your opinions with reasons.

Axelrod's Claims Regarding FDR	Evidence Axelrod Uses for Support	My Thoughts: Is the Evidence Relevant and Sufficient to Support the Claims? Why or Why Not?
		(Circle 1) Yes No Why or why not:
		(Circle 1) Yes No Why or why not:
		(Circle 1) Yes No Why or why not:
		(Circle 1) Yes No Why or why not:

Name _____ Date _____

from Americans in the Great Depression by Eric Rauchway
Vocabulary Builder

Selection Vocabulary

disproportionately   prevalence   solicitude

A. DIRECTIONS: *Write the letter of the word or phrase that is the best synonym for the italicized word.*

_____ 1. *disproportionately*
   A. unexpectedly
   B. not widely accepted
   C. not equally
   D. not possibly

_____ 2. *solicitude*
   A. the state of being silent
   B. the state of being in charge
   C. the state of being overworked
   D. the state of being worried

_____ 3. *prevalence*
   A. awareness
   B. existence in large numbers
   C. having great value
   D. existence in poor condition

Academic Vocabulary

establish   devastation   illuminate

B. DIRECTIONS: *Write a response to each question. Make sure to use the word in italics at least once in your response.*

1. What piece of evidence might be used to *illuminate* this statement?
   He is a very generous man.
   _____

2. What might a politician do to *establish* his or her reputation as an honest person?
   _____

3. What type of event in nature might cause *devastation*?
   _____

All-in-One Workbook
© Pearson Education, Inc. All rights reserved.

Name _____ Date _____

from **Americans in the Great Depression** by Eric Rauchway
Take Notes for Discussion

Before the Partner Discussion: Read the following passage from the selection.

> As one sociologist wrote, "The average American has the feeling that work . . . is the only dignified way of life. . . . While theoretically, economic activities are supposed to be the means to the good life, as a matter of fact it is not the end, but the means themselves, that have the greater prestige."

During the Discussion: As you present your views and listen to those of your partner, take notes on how his or her ideas either differ from or build upon your own.

Discussion Questions	Other Ideas Expressed	Comparison to My Own Ideas
1. How did circumstances during the Great Depression make this a particularly difficult—even damaging—attitude?		
2. Do you think most Americans still hold this attitude today? Explain.		

All-in-One Workbook

Name _____ Date _____

from **Americans in the Great Depression** by Eric Rauchway
Take Notes for Research

As you research **ways in which the drought in the Great Plains, which resulted in the Dust Bowl, contributed to the Great Depression,** use the organizer below to take notes from your sources. As necessary, continue your notes on the back of this page, on note cards, or in a word-processing document.

How the Drought and the Dust Bowl Contributed to the Great Depression	
Main Idea _____ Quotation or Paraphrase _____ Source Information _____ 	Main Idea _____ Quotation or Paraphrase _____ Source Information _____
Main Idea _____ Quotation or Paraphrase _____ Source Information _____ 	Main Idea _____ Quotation or Paraphrase _____ Source Information _____

Name _____ Date _____

from **Americans in the Great Depression** by Eric Rauchway
Take Notes for Writing to Sources

Planning Your Narrative: Before you begin drafting your **fictional narrative,** use the chart below to organize your ideas. Follow the directions at the top of each box.

1. Introduce the main character. Use details from the text to describe how he or she was affected by the Great Depression.
_____
_____
_____
_____
_____

2. Step into the shoes of this character. Build a first-person narrative to describe the setting and the conflicts you face. Base your narrative on facts and details from the text.
_____
_____
_____
_____
_____
_____
_____
_____

3. Draft pieces of realistic dialogue to make your narrative seem authentic.
_____
_____
_____
_____
_____
_____

4. Draft a conclusion to the narrative. Show how the conflicts and hardships of the Great Depression will affect his or her attitude toward the future.
_____
_____
_____
_____
_____
_____

Name _____ Date _____

from Women on the Breadlines, by Meridel Le Sueur
Vocabulary Builder

Selection Vocabulary

    exodus   futility   privations

A. DIRECTIONS: *Complete each sentence with a word, phrase, or clause that contains a context clue for the italicized word.*

1. Due to the severe drought, the farmers decided to join others in an *exodus* that _____
   _____

2. Society should help those with *privations* by taking such steps as _____
   _____

3. The *futility* of our efforts to stop the rising flood waters became obvious when _____
   _____

Academic Vocabulary

    articulate   interaction   subjective

B. DIRECTIONS: *Revise each sentence so that the underlined vocabulary word is used logically. Be sure not to change the vocabulary word.*

1. She is quite <u>articulate</u> and is even more tongue-tied than her sister.
   _____

2. Because the two characters never met, they had a great deal of <u>interaction</u>.
   _____

3. His news reports provide facts, not his opinions, and they are praised for being completely <u>subjective</u>.
   _____

Name _____ Date _____

from Women on the Breadlines, by Meridel Le Sueur
Take Notes for Discussion

Before the Group Discussion: Read the following passage from the selection.

Hunger makes a human being lapse into a state of lethargy, especially city hunger. Is there any place else in the world where a human being is supposed to go hungry amidst plenty without an outcry, without protest, where only the boldest steal or kill for bread, and the timid crawl the streets, hunger like the beak of a terrible bird at the vitals?

During the Discussion: As you present your views and listen to those of other students, take notes on how their ideas either differ from or build upon your own.

Discussion Questions	Other Ideas Expressed	Comparison to My Own Ideas
1. Do you agree that being hungry in a city is, somehow, worse than being hungry in the country?		
2. What does Le Sueur's distinction between the "boldest" and the "timid" suggest about human nature in times of crisis?		

Name _____ Date _____

from Women on the Breadlines, by Meridel Le Sueur
Take Notes for Research

As you research **the value of the dollar and what poverty and wealth meant in dollar amounts during the Depression,** use the organizer below to take notes from your sources. As necessary, continue your notes on the back of this page, on note cards, or in a word-processing document.

The Value of the Dollar During the Great Depression, and What Poverty and Wealth Meant in Dollar Amounts

Main Idea _____

Quotation or Paraphrase _____

Source Information _____

Main Idea _____

Quotation or Paraphrase _____

Source Information _____

Main Idea _____

Quotation or Paraphrase _____

Source Information _____

Main Idea _____

Quotation or Paraphrase _____

Source Information _____

All-in-One Workbook

Name _____ Date _____

from Women on the Breadlines, by Meridel Le Sueur
Take Notes for Writing to Sources

Planning Your Explanation: Before you begin drafting your **explanatory essay,** use the chart below to organize your ideas. Then use your notes to describe and summarize the challenges and hardships that many urban women faced during the Great Depression.

Le Sueur's Premise: Women endured hardships that men generally did not.	
Facts and Details from the Text	**How Will the Facts and Details Be Helpful in My Explanation?**
	(Circle one) Yes No Why or why not:
	(Circle one) Yes No Why or why not:
	(Circle one) Yes No Why or why not:
	(Circle one) Yes No Why or why not:
	(Circle one) Yes No Why or why not:
	(Circle one) Yes No Why or why not:

Name _____ Date _____

"Bread Line, New York City, 1932" by H. W. Fechner
Vocabulary Builder and Take Notes for Writing to Sources

Academic Vocabulary

composition   elevated   objective

DIRECTIONS: *Complete each sentence with a word, phrase, or clause that contains a context clue for the underlined word.*

1. The composition of the photograph was very dramatic because _____
   _____

2. By choosing an elevated place to stand while watching the parade, we _____
   _____

3. Try to be objective when you answer the question. In other words, _____
   _____

Take Notes for Writing to Sources

Planning Your Explanation: Before you begin drafting your **explanatory caption,** use the diagram below to organize your ideas. Jot down notes in each outer box.

Details about the season:	The photo captures the severe hunger that many people faced during the Depression.	Details about the people:

Details about the location:

All-in-One Workbook
© Pearson Education, Inc. All rights reserved.

Name _____ Date _____

Unit 3: Poetry
Big Question Vocabulary—1

 The Big Question: How does communication change us?

Honest and frequent communication is important to keep relationships healthy. When you are in doubt about the meaning of somebody's words or actions, the best thing to do is open a dialogue with him or her and ask.

discuss: to talk about something and exchange ideas

empathy: understanding and identifying with another's feelings

interpretation: an explanation or understanding of something

relationship: a connection or association between people

resolution: a final solution to a problem or difficulty

DIRECTIONS: *Leave a message on the answering machine of a close friend or relative, telling them that you want to talk about something he or she did that upset you. Use all of the vocabulary words.*

Name _____ Date _____

Unit 3: Poetry
Big Question Vocabulary—2

The Big Question: How does communication change us?

When we read a newspaper or watch television, we receive information, but we do not usually contribute information. In some cases, though, it is possible to take some action that communicates a message in response to news.

communication: the act of speaking or writing to share ideas

comprehension: the ability to understand something

informed: having knowledge gained through study, communication, research, and so on

respond: to reply; to react favorably

understanding: *n.* a grasp of the meaning of something;
        adj. having compassion or showing sympathy

DIRECTIONS: *Think about a news story or issue that you care about, and then answer the questions below. Use the vocabulary words in parentheses in each of your answers.*

1. Where did you hear about the news story or issue? (*communication*)
   _____
   _____
   _____

2. What new knowledge did you gain when you heard the story or issue? (*informed*)
   _____
   _____
   _____

3. What are you confused about related to the story or issue? (*understanding*)
   _____
   _____
   _____

4. What would clarify the story for you? (*comprehension*)
   _____
   _____
   _____

5. Is there any action you can take to improve or change this issue? (*respond*)
   _____
   _____
   _____

Name _____ Date _____

Unit 3: Poetry
Big Question Vocabulary—3

 The Big Question: How does communication change us?

Sometimes a conversation with someone can cause you to understand things in a new way and, as a result, take action.

aware: informed; knowledgeable

exchange: to give something for something else, as in an exchange of ideas

illuminate: to make clear; to give light to

meaning: what is expressed or what is intended to be expressed; the purpose or significance of something

react: to act in response to an agent or influence

DIRECTIONS: *Use the vocabulary words to help Douglas understand the newspaper strike.*

Douglas had no idea why his paper was not delivered this morning. It had ruined his morning. On his way to work, he stopped at a newsstand and was told about a strike at the newspaper office. Sure enough, as he passed the newspaper office, there were picketers, holding signs.

One of the picketers stopped Douglas and asked him to sign a petition to help the newspaper staff get a raise in pay.

They had the following conversation:

Douglas:

Striker:

Douglas:

Striker:

All-in-One Workbook
© Pearson Education, Inc. All rights reserved.
118

Name _____ Date _____

Unit 3: Poetry
Applying the Big Question

The Big Question: How does communication change us?

DIRECTIONS: Complete the chart below to apply what you have learned about communication. One row has been completed for you.

Example	The subject	What happens	The writer's response	How my ideas changed
From Literature	Making decisions in "The Road Not Taken"	The speaker makes a decision about a small matter.	The decision may change his life forever.	I realize that small decisions may affect my entire life.
From Literature				
From Science				
From Social Studies				
From Real Life				

All-in-One Workbook
© Pearson Education, Inc. All rights reserved.

Name _____ Date _____

Poetry Collection: Langston Hughes, Emily Dickinson, Gabriela Mistral, Jean de Sponde

Writing About the Big Question

 How does communication change us?

Big Question Vocabulary

aware	communication	comprehension	discuss	empathy
exchange	illuminate	informed	interpretation	meaning
react	relationship	resolution	respond	understanding

A. *Use one or more words from the list above to complete each sentence.*

1. Two people who do not speak the same language may find _____ difficult.

2. Because we shared their feelings deeply, we wanted to communicate our _____ to them.

3. A good dictionary is a valuable resource for determining the _____ of an unfamiliar word.

4. Sometimes you need courage and patience when you _____ a difficult issue or conflict with others.

5. To communicate with others effectively, you need to remain _____ of their point of view.

B. *Follow the directions in responding to each of the items below.*

1. List two different times when you have found **communication** with another person difficult.
   _____
   _____

2. Write two sentences to explain one of these experiences, and describe how it made you feel. Use at least two of the Big Question vocabulary words.
   _____
   _____

C. *Complete the sentence below. Then, write a short paragraph in which you connect the sentence to the Big Question.*

When the speaker of a poem asks the audience to **respond** to a question, the audience is encouraged to _____
_____
_____
_____

All-in-One Workbook
© Pearson Education, Inc. All rights reserved.

Name _____ Date _____

Poetry Collection: Langston Hughes, Emily Dickinson,
Gabriela Mistral, Jean de Sponde

Literary Analysis: Figurative Language

Figurative language is language that is used imaginatively rather than literally. Figurative language includes one or more **figures of speech,** literary devices that make unexpected comparisons or change the usual meanings of words. The following are figures of speech:

- **Simile:** a comparison of two apparently unlike things using *like, as, than,* or *resembles*
- **Metaphor:** a comparison of two apparently unlike things without using *like, as, than,* or *resembles*
- **Personification:** giving human characteristics to a nonhuman subject
- **Paradox:** a statement, an idea, or a situation that seems contradictory but actually expresses a truth

DIRECTIONS: *Read the following passages and then use the lines provided to identify each example of figurative language. Briefly indicate the reason for your answer.*

1. "Does it stink like rotten meat?" ("Dream Deferred")
   _____
   _____

2. "Life is a broken-winged bird / That cannot fly." ("Dreams")
   _____
   _____

3. "I've heard it in the chillest land—
   And on the strangest Sea—
   Yet, never, in Extremity,
   It asked a crumb—of Me." ("Hope is the thing with feathers—")
   _____
   _____

4. "The wind wandering by night
   rocks the wheat.
   Hearing the loving wind
   I rock my son." ("Rocking")
   _____
   _____

5. "What becomes more and more secure, the longer
   it is battered by inconstancy . . .?" ("Sonnet on Love XIII")
   _____
   _____

All-in-One Workbook

Name _____ Date _____

Poetry Collection: Langston Hughes, Emily Dickinson,
Gabriela Mistral, Jean de Sponde

Reading: Read Fluently

Reading fluently is reading smoothly and continuously while also comprehending the text and appreciating the writer's artistry. To improve your fluency when reading poetry, **read in sentences.** Use punctuation—periods, commas, colons, semicolons, and dashes—rather than the ends of lines to determine where to pause or stop reading.

DIRECTIONS: *Read the following passages and then answer the questions on the lines provided.*

1. "God, the Father, soundlessly rocks
   his thousands of worlds.
   Feeling His hand in the shadow
   I rock my son." ("Rocking")

   At the ends of which lines would you make major pauses in reading? Would you pause briefly at the end of the first or third line even though there is no punctuation? Why or why not?

   _____
   _____

2. "But if that dead
   sage could return to life, he would find a clear
   demonstration of his idea, which is not
   pure theory after all. That putative spot
   exists in the love I feel for you, my dear." ("Sonnet on Love XIII")

   After which words would you make a minor pause? After which words would you make a major pause?

   _____
   _____

3. "Does it dry up
   like a raisin in the sun?
   "Or fester like a sore—
   And then run?

   Maybe it just sags
   like a heavy load." ("A Dream Deferred")

   After which words at the end of lines should you not make any pause at all?

   _____
   _____

All-in-One Workbook
© Pearson Education, Inc. All rights reserved.

Name _____ Date _____

Poetry Collection: Langston Hughes, Emily Dickinson,
Gabriela Mistral, Jean de Sponde

Vocabulary Builder

Word List

barren   deferred   fester   paradoxical   abash

A. DIRECTIONS: *Answer each of the following questions.*

___ 1. Which of the following is the best synonym for *deferred*?
    A. postponed   B. analyzed   C. replaced   D. completed

___ 2. Which of the following most nearly means the opposite of *paradoxical*?
    A. deliberate   B. thoughtless   C. contradictory   D. agreeing

___ 3. Which of the following is the best synonym for *barren*?
    A. plentiful   B. sterile   C. elegant   D. wealthy

___ 4. Which of the following most nearly means the opposite of *fester*?
    A. frighten   B. heal   C. scar   D. relax

B. DIRECTIONS: *For each of the following items, think about the meaning of the italicized word and then answer the question.*

1. Would playing a song in the wrong key likely *abash* a musician? Why or why not?
   _____

2. Would you be happy if your salary or the fee for a job you had completed was unexpectedly *deferred*? Why or why not?
   _____

3. Would a *paradoxical* statement be easy to understand at first? Why or why not?
   _____

4. If a wound is allowed to *fester*, will it heal quickly? Why or why not?
   _____

C. WORD STUDY: *Match the word with the latin root -fer- in Column A with its meaning in Column B by writing the correct letter on the line provided.*

___ 1. transfer   A. meet with
___ 2. conifer   B. carry across
___ 3. confer   C. greater liking
___ 4. preference   D. pine or spruce tree

Name _____ Date _____

Poetry Collection 1: Langston Hughes, Gabriela Mistral,
Jean de Sponde, Emily Dickinson

Conventions: Prepositions and Prepositional Phrases

A **preposition** is a word that relates a noun or pronoun that appears with it to another word in the sentence. Although most prepositions, such as *at, by, in,* and *with,* are single words, some prepositions, such as *because of* and *in addition to,* are compound. In the following example from "Rocking," the prepositions are in italics.

"God, the Father, soundlessly rocks
His thousands *of* worlds.
Feeling His hand *in* the shadow
I rock my son."

The **object of a preposition** is the noun or pronoun at the end of a prepositional phrase. In the following example, the prepositional phrase is underlined and the object of the preposition is in italics.

Gabriela Mistral wrote many poems <u>about *children*</u>.

A. PRACTICE: *Read the following passages from the poems in this collection. On the lines provided, write each prepositional phrase. Then, circle the object of the preposition.*

1. "'Hope is the thing with feathers—
   That perches in the soul—"
   _____

2. "Hold fast to dreams
   For when dreams go
   Life is a barren field
   Frozen with snow."
   _____

3. "That putative spot
   exists in the love I feel for you, my dear."
   _____

B. Writing Application: *Write a brief paragraph in which you describe the way you get to school in the morning. Use at least five prepositional phrases in your writing, and underline each prepositional phrase you use.*

_____
_____
_____
_____
_____

Name _____ Date _____

Poetry Collection 1: Langston Hughes, Gabriela Mistral, Jean de Sponde, Emily Dickinson

Support for Writing to Sources: Informative Text

Use the following lines to make prewriting notes for your description of a scene in nature.

Choice of Scene: _____
_____

Sensory Details:

1. **Sight:** _____
_____
_____

2. **Sound:** _____
_____
_____

3. **Touch:** _____
_____
_____

4. **Smell:** _____
_____
_____

5. **Taste:** _____
_____
_____

Unified Impression: _____
_____

Now, use your notes to write a few paragraphs or a poem describing a scene in nature.

Name _____ Date _____

Poetry Collection 1: Langston Hughes, Gabriela Mistral,
Jean de Sponde, and Emily Dickinson

Support for Speaking and Listening: Speech

Use the following lines to make prewriting notes for your impromptu speech about dreams, nature, or love.

My Speech Topic: _____
_____

My Central Idea: _____
_____
_____
_____

Ideas for Body Language and Eye Contact: _____
_____
_____
_____
_____
_____

My Conclusion: _____
_____
_____
_____
_____
_____

Name _____ Date _____

Poetry Collection: Edgar Allan Poe, May Swenson, Yusef Komunyakaa, Lewis Carroll

Writing About the Big Question

How does communication change us?

Big Question Vocabulary

aware	communication	comprehension	discuss	empathy
exchange	illuminate	informed	interpretation	meaning
react	relationship	resolution	respond	understanding

A. *Use one or more words from the list above to complete each sentence.*

1. Most of us _____ favorably when someone invites us to a party.

2. For good _____ in a foreign country, some knowledge of the language is helpful.

3. The committee met several times to _____ that issue before it made a final decision.

4. Otto was a man of few words, and it was sometimes hard to figure out his real _____.

5. Thelma's _____ of the poem had never occurred to me, but I had to admit that it made sense.

B. *Follow the directions in responding to each of the items below.*

1. List two different times when you had a disagreement with a friend.
   _____
   _____

2. Write two sentences to explain one of these experiences, and describe how it made you feel. Use at least two of the Big Question vocabulary words.
   _____
   _____

C. *Complete the sentence below. Then, write a short paragraph in which you connect the sentence to the Big Question.*

By reading about the **meaning** that someone finds in certain sounds, a reader can learn to _____
_____
_____
_____
_____

All-in-One Workbook
© Pearson Education, Inc. All rights reserved.

Name _____ Date _____

Poetry Collection: Yusef Komunyakaa, Lewis Carroll, Edgar Allan Poe, May Swenson
Literary Analysis: Sound Devices

Poets use **sound devices** to emphasize the sound relationships among words. These devices include the following:

- **Alliteration:** the repetition of initial consonant sounds in stressed syllables: "<u>m</u>uffled <u>m</u>onotone"
- **Consonance:** the repetition of final consonant sounds in stressed syllables with different vowel sounds, as in *toll* and *bell*
- **Assonance:** the repetition of similar vowel sounds in stressed syllables that end with different consonant sounds, as in "*mellow wedding bells*"
- **Onomatopoeia:** the use of a word whose sound imitates its meaning, as in *jangle* and *knells*

DIRECTIONS: *Analyze each poem. For each poem, give one or more examples of each of the following sound devices. If a poem does not use a particular sound device, write* None.

Sound Device	"Slam, Dunk, & Hook"	"Jabberwocky"	"The Bells"	"Analysis of Baseball"
Alliteration				
Assonance				
Consonance				
Onomatopoeia				

Name _____ Date _____

Poetry Collection: Yusef Komunyakaa, Lewis Carroll, Edgar Allan Poe, May Swenson

Reading: Read Fluently

Reading fluently is reading smoothly and continuously while also comprehending the text and appreciating the writer's craft. You may need to read poems several times to unlock their layers of meaning.

- First Reading: Read for basic meaning.
- Second Reading: Read to unlock deeper meanings.
- Third Reading: Read to recognize and appreciate the poet's craft.

DIRECTIONS: *Choose one poem in this collection and read it three times, changing your focus as you read. Jot down notes on what you better understand each time.*

Poem:	My Understanding
1st Reading • Read for basic meaning	
2nd Reading • Read to unlock deeper meanings.	
3rd Reading • Read to recognize and appreciate the poet's craft.	

Name _____ Date _____

Poetry Collection: Yusef Komunyakaa, Lewis Carroll, Edgar Allan Poe, May Swenson
Vocabulary Builder

Word List

disgrace   endeavor   jibed   metaphysical
monotone   palpitating   voluminously

A. DIRECTIONS: Match each word in Column A with the correct definition in Column B.

Column A	Column B
___ 1. metaphysical	A. serious attempt
___ 2. palpitating	B. spiritual
___ 3. voluminously	C. loss of respect
___ 4. jibed	D. throbbing
___ 5. endeavor	E. fully
___ 6. disgrace	F. changed direction

B. DIRECTIONS: Revise each sentence so that the italicized vocabulary word is used logically. Be sure not to change the vocabulary word.

1. He spoke in a *monotone*, full of delightful and surprising shifts in tone and mood.
   _____

2. She was determined in her *endeavor* to finish the assignment that night, so she went to bed early.
   _____

3. My heart was *palpitating* from the soothing music.
   _____

C. WORD STUDY: Use the context of the sentences and what you know about the Greek prefix *mono-* to explain your answer to each question.

1. If the animals of a certain species are *monogamous*, do they have one mate or many?
   _____
   _____

2. Is a person with *monomania* interested in one subject or in many?
   _____
   _____

3. In a play, is a *monologue* spoken by one character or by many?
   _____
   _____

Poetry Collection: Yusef Komunyakaa, Lewis Carroll, Edgar Allan Poe, and May Swenson

Conventions: Participles and Participial Phrases, Gerunds and Gerund Phrases

Participles and Participial Phrases

A **participle** is a verb form that acts as an adjective.

There are two kinds of participles: present participles and past participles. **Present participles** end in -ing. The **past participles** of regular verbs end in -ed.

A **participial phrase** is a participle and any modifiers, object or complement; the entire phrase acts as an adjective.

Participle:	She glimpsed a *soaring* eagle. (modifies *eagle*)
Participial Phrase:	She glimpsed a bird *soaring high in the sky*. (modifies *bird*)

A. DIRECTIONS: *In the following sentences, identify each participle or participial phrase. Indicate the word each one modifies.*

1. On the third strike, swinging at the pitcher's fast ball, the batter struck out.

2. Scoring twenty-four points, Yusef was the most valuable player of that game.

3. Ringing bells echo through the town.

Gerunds and Gerund Phrases

A **gerund** is a form of a verb that acts as a noun. It can function as a subject, an object of a verb or preposition, or a predicate noun. A **gerund phrase** is a gerund and any modifiers, object, or complement; the entire phrase acts as a noun.

Look at the following examples:

Gerund:	*Singing* was a delight. (subject)
Gerund Phrase:	*Singing with the community chorus* was a way to make new friends. (subject)
	We always took pleasure in *attending the rehearsals on Friday nights*. (object of preposition)

B. DIRECTIONS: *In the following sentences, identify each gerund or gerund phrase, and identify its function.*

1. Rehearsing weekly was a necessity.

2. For weeks, we worked toward the goal of presenting a special Thanksgiving concert.

3. Maria practices playing the piano for several hours each day.

Name _____ Date _____

Poetry Collection: May Swenson, Yusef Komunyakaa,
Lewis Carroll, Edgar Allan Poe

Support for Writing to Sources: Argument

Use the following chart to develop prewriting notes for an editorial that will be related to a poem in this collection.

Title of Poem: _____

Issue or Topic Related to Poem: _____
_____
_____

My Opinion Statement: _____
_____
_____
_____

Supporting Details:

1. _____
_____

2. _____
_____

3. _____
_____

4. _____
_____

5. _____
_____

Opposing Arguments / Counterarguments:
_____
_____
_____
_____

Now, use your notes to write an editorial about the issue you have chosen.

Name _____ Date _____

Poetry Collection 2: May Swenson, Yusef Komunyakaa, Lewis Carroll, and Edgar Allan Poe
Support for Speaking and Listening: Illustrated Presentation

Together with your group, use a format such as the one shown to develop an illustrated presentation of one of the poems in this collection.

Title of Poem: _____

Images That Capture Poem's Mood: _____
_____
_____
_____
_____
_____
_____

Ideas for Photographs/Artwork: _____
_____
_____
_____
_____
_____
_____

Now use your notes to develop an illustrated presentation of a poem in this collection.

All-in-One Workbook
© Pearson Education, Inc. All rights reserved.

Name _____ Date _____

Poetry Collection: Ernest Lawrence Thayer, William Stafford, Sandra Cisneros, Edgar Allan Poe

Writing About the Big Question

 How does communication change us?

Big Question Vocabulary

aware	communication	comprehension	discuss	empathy
exchange	illuminate	informed	interpretation	meaning
react	relationship	resolution	respond	understanding

A. *Use one or more words from the list above to complete each sentence.*

1. The chairperson announced, "We will not reach a _____ in this debate unless we all listen carefully to one another's viewpoints."

2. My _____ with Ken was damaged when I learned he was telling lies about me.

3. "It is my _____," Stacy said, "that the package will arrive at our office before 2 P.M."

4. "Let's _____ e-mail addresses," Matt urged, "so we can stay in touch."

5. That article helped a lot to _____ some obscure passages in the poem.

B. *Follow the directions in responding to each of the items below.*

1. List two different times when an **exchange** of ideas with someone else persuaded you to change your mind about someone or something.
   _____
   _____

2. Write two sentences to explain one of these experiences, and describe how it made you feel. Use at least two of the Big Question vocabulary words.
   _____
   _____

C. *Complete the sentence below. Then, write a short paragraph in which you connect the sentence to the Big Question.*

When a crowd communicates its support or disapproval, a person might **react** by
_____
_____
_____

All-in-One Workbook

Name _____ Date _____

Poetry Collection: Ernest Lawrence Thayer, William Stafford,
Sandra Cisneros, and Edgar Allan Poe

Literary Analysis: Narrative Poetry

Narrative poetry is verse that tells a story and includes the same literary elements as narrative prose: a plot, or sequence of events; specific settings; characters who participate in the action. Also like narrative prose, such as a short story, a narrative poem conveys a **mood,** or **atmosphere**—an overall feeling created by the setting, plot, words, and images. For example, a narrative poem's mood can be gloomy, joyous, or mysterious. Poetry's emphasis on precise words and images makes mood a powerful element in a narrative poem.

DIRECTIONS: *As you read the poems in this collection, answer the following questions.*

"Casey at the Bat"

1. What story does this poem tell?
   _____

2. Who are the two most important characters in the poem?
   _____

3. Briefly describe the poem's outcome.
   _____

4. How does Thayer use details of sound to contribute to the poem's setting?
   _____
   _____

"Fifteen"

5. Who is the speaker in this poem, and what occasion does he recall?
   _____

6. What is the principal conflict in "Fifteen"?
   _____

"Twister Hits Houston"

7. What details create suspense in this narrative poem?
   _____

8. How would you describe the atmosphere, or mood, at the end of the poem?
   _____

"The Raven"

9. Who is the speaker in the poem? What kind of person is this speaker?
   _____

10. Briefly describe the poem's setting.
    _____

11. What story does the poem tell?
    _____

Name _____ Date _____

Poetry Collection: Ernest Lawrence Thayer, William Stafford,
Sandra Cisneros, and Edgar Allan Poe

Reading: Paraphrasing

Paraphrasing is restating in your own words what someone else has written or said. A paraphrase retains the essential meaning and ideas of the original but is simpler to read.

Paraphrasing is especially helpful when reading poetry because poems often contain **figurative language,** words and phrases that are used imaginatively rather than literally. To paraphrase lines in a narrative poem, **picture the action:** Based on details in the poem, form a mental image of the setting, the characters, and the characters' actions. To be sure that your mental picture is accurate, pay close attention to the way that the poet describes elements of the scene. Then, use your own words to describe your mental image of the scene and the action taking place in it.

DIRECTIONS: *On the lines provided, paraphrase the following passages from the narrative poems in this collection. Remember that a paraphrase is a restatement in your own words.*

1. And now the leather-covered sphere came hurtling through the air,
   And Casey stood a-watching it in haughty grandeur there.
   Close by the sturdy batsman the ball unheeded sped;
   "That ain't my style," said Casey. "Strike one," the umpire said. ("Casey at the Bat")

   _____
   _____

2. I admired all that pulsing gleam, the
   shiny flanks, the demure headlights,
   fringed where it lay; I led it gently
   to the road and stood with that
   companion, ready and friendly. I was fifteen. ("Fifteen")

   _____
   _____

3. Papa who was sitting on his front porch
   when the storm hit
   said the twister ripped
   the big black oak to splinter . . . ("Twister Hits Houston")

   _____
   _____

4. Eagerly I wished the morrow—vainly I had tried to borrow
   From my books surcease of sorrow—sorrow for the lost Lenore—
   For the rare and radiant maiden whom the angels name Lenore—
       Nameless here for evermore ("The Raven")

   _____
   _____

Name _____ Date _____

Poetry Collection: Ernest Lawrence Thayer, William Stafford, Sandra Cisneros, and Edgar Allan Poe

Vocabulary Builder

Word List

beguiling   defiance   demure   multitude
pallor   pondered   preceded   respite   writhing

A. Directions: Match each word in Column A with the correct definition in Column B.

Column A
___ 1. pallor
___ 2. writhing
___ 3. demure
___ 4. pondered
___ 5. beguiling

Column B
A. twisting
B. thought deeply about
C. paleness
D. modest
E. tricking

B. Directions: In each of the following items, think about the meaning of the italicized word and then answer the question.

1. A *multitude* viewed the parade. Why might it have been hard to see the marchers?
   _____

2. Jean reacted with *defiance* when we politely asked her to be quiet during the speech. Why might we have felt annoyed?
   _____

3. At ten o'clock we took a *respite* from work. Did we keep working at ten o'clock? Explain.
   _____

C. Word Study: Use the context of each sentence and what you know about the Latin prefix *pre-* to rewrite the sentence so that it makes sense. Be careful not to change the word in italics.

1. Lucy was greatly interested in the comments by the authors in the *preface* at the end of the report.
   _____
   _____

2. The mayor marched last in the parade; she *preceded* all the other marchers.
   _____
   _____

3. Thinking about yesterday's history test, Mark has a *premonition* that several questions would relate to the chapter review.
   _____
   _____

Poetry Collection 3: Ernest Lawrence Thayer, William Stafford, Sandra Cisneros, Edgar Allan Poe

Conventions: Appositive and Absolute Phrases

An **appositive** is a noun or pronoun placed near another noun or pronoun to identify, rename, or explain it. Notice in the following example that the appositive is set off by commas, which indicates that it is not essential to the meaning of the sentence and can be removed.

Example: The author of "The Raven," *Edgar Allan Poe,* was also a noted short-story writer.

In the following example, the appositive *Edgar Allan Poe* is not set off by commas because it is needed to complete the meaning of the sentence.

Example: The American writer *Edgar Allan Poe* may have invented the modern short story.

When an appositive has its own modifiers, it forms an **appositive phrase.** Appositive phrases are placed next to a noun or pronoun to add information and details.

Example: We enjoyed reading "The Cask of Amontillado," *a thrilling tale of suspense.*

An **absolute phrase** adds information to an entire sentence. It consists of a noun or a pronoun followed by a participle and its object, complement, and/or modifiers. An absolute phrase often *looks* like a sentence, but it cannot stand alone.

Example: The raven stared at me, *its black eyes filling me with dread.*
Example: *The sound growing louder,* the man trembled in fear.

A. Practice: *Underline the appositive phrase or the absolute phrase in each of the following sentences. Then, after each sentence, write whether it is an* appositive phrase *or an* absolute phrase.

1. His descriptions featuring deliberate exaggerations, the author uses hyperbole to achieve an effect.

2. Homer, the oral poet credited with composing the *Iliad* and the *Odyssey*, often uses hyperbole to describe the deeds of epic heroes.

3. Jonathan Swift employs the same device for fantastic effects in *Gulliver's Travels*, his pointed satire on human life and behavior.

B. Writing Application: *Write a brief paragraph in which you describe an appliance that you often use at home. Use one or more appositive phrases and one or more absolute phrases in your writing, and underline each appositive and absolute phrase you use.*

_____
_____
_____
_____
_____
_____
_____

Name _____ Date _____

Poetry Collection: Ernest Lawrence Thayer, William Stafford, Sandra Cisneros, Edgar Allan Poe

Support for Writing to Sources: Informative Text

For your movie scene, use the following lines to make notes.

Details from the poem

1. **Characters:** _____
_____

2. **Setting:** _____
_____

3. **Actions:** _____
_____

4. **Mood:** _____
_____

Mood in Movie's Opening Scene: _____
_____
_____
_____
_____

Details Contributing to Mood: _____
_____
_____
_____
_____
_____

Camera Angles, Lighting, and so on: _____
_____
_____
_____
_____

Name _____   Date _____

Poetry Collection: Ernest Lawrence Thayer, William Stafford,
Sandra Cisneros, Edgar Allan Poe

Support for Speaking and Listening: Dialogue

Use the following lines to take notes for your dialogue between the speaker and the motorcyclist in "Fifteen" or between Papa and Mama in "Twister Hits Houston."

Details in Poem About Character, Setting, and Action:

_____
_____
_____
_____

Main Concerns of Participants in Dialogue:

Main Concerns of Character A:

_____
_____
_____
_____

Main Concerns of Character B:

_____
_____
_____
_____

What we learn about their relationship:

_____
_____
_____
_____

All-in-One Workbook
© Pearson Education, Inc. All rights reserved.

Name _____   Date _____

Poetry Collection: Emily Dickinson, Robert Frost, T. S. Eliot, William Shakespeare

Writing About the Big Question

How does communication change us?

Big Question Vocabulary

aware	communication	comprehension	discuss	empathy
exchange	illuminate	informed	interpretation	meaning
react	relationship	resolution	respond	understanding

A. *Use one or more words from the list above to complete each sentence.*

1. Although the Martinez family spent a year away in Spain, we stayed in regular _____ with them by e-mail.

2. In order to _____ ideas effectively, you need to listen carefully to the other group members.

3. The twin sisters' _____ is so close that one can usually tell what the other is thinking, even without speaking.

4. In an oral presentation, graphic aids like charts can help you _____ your _____ for the audience.

B. *Follow the directions in responding to each of the items below.*

1. List two different times when good **communication** with another person helped you solve a problem or overcome a challenge.
   _____
   _____

2. Write two sentences to explain one of these experiences, and describe how it made you feel. Use at least two of the Big Question vocabulary words.
   _____
   _____

C. *Complete the sentence below. Then, write a short paragraph in which you connect the sentence to the Big Question.*

Other people can make someone **aware** of his or her potential by _____
_____
_____
_____
_____
_____

All-in-One Workbook
© Pearson Education, Inc. All rights reserved.

Name _____ Date _____

Poetry Collection: Robert Frost, Emily Dickinson, T. S. Eliot, and William Shakespeare
Literary Analysis: Rhyme and Meter

Rhyme is the repetition of sounds at the ends of words. There are several types of rhyme:

- **Exact rhyme:** the repetition of words that end with the same vowel and consonant sounds, as in *end* and *mend*
- **Slant rhyme:** the repetition of words that end with similar sounds but do not rhyme perfectly, as in *end* and *stand*
- **End rhyme:** the rhyming sounds of words at the ends of lines
- **Internal rhyme:** the rhyming of words within a line

A **rhyme scheme** is a regular pattern of end rhymes in a poem or stanza. A rhyme scheme is described by assigning one letter of the alphabet to each rhyming sound. For example, in "Uphill" by Christina Rossetti, the rhyme scheme is *abab*:

Does the road wind uphill all the <u>way</u>?   *a*
   Yes, to the very <u>end</u>.   *b*
Will the day's journey take the whole long <u>day</u>?   *a*
   From morn to night, my <u>friend</u>.   *b*

Meter is the rhythmical pattern in a line of poetry. Meter results from the arrangement of stressed (´) and unstressed (˘) syllables. When you read aloud a line with a regular meter, you can hear the steady, rhythmic pulse of the stressed syllables:

"and maggie discovered a shell that sang"
"Let not Ambition mock their useful toil"

Not all poems include rhyme, a rhyme scheme, or a regular meter. However, poets often use one or more of these techniques to create musical effects and achieve a sense of unity.

DIRECTIONS: *Read this stanza from "Dream Variations," a poem by Langston Hughes. Identify the rhyme scheme and think about how it emphasizes the speaker's meaning. Also think about Hughes's use of meter in these lines. Then, answer the questions on the lines provided.*

    To fling my arms wide
    In some place of the sun,
    To whirl and to dance
    Till the white day is done.
5   Then rest at cool evening
    Beneath a tall tree
    While night comes on gently,
      Dark like me—
    That is my dream!

1. What is the rhyme scheme of this stanza?

_____

2. How does the rhyme scheme help to set off the last line in the stanza?

_____

3. Is the meter in these lines regular or irregular? Explain your answer.

_____

Name _____ Date _____

Poetry Collection: Robert Frost, Emily Dickinson, T. S. Eliot, and William Shakespeare
Reading: Paraphrasing

Paraphrasing is restating in your own words what someone else has written or said. A paraphrase should retain the essential meaning and ideas of the original but should be simpler to read. One way to simplify the text that you are paraphrasing is to **break down long sentences,** dividing long sentences into parts and paraphrasing those parts. Poets often write sentences that span several lines to give their poems fluidity. By breaking down long sentences and paraphrasing them, you can enjoy a poem's fluid quality without missing its meaning.

DIRECTIONS: *Paraphrase the following passages from the poems in this collection.*

1. Then took the other, as just as fair,
   And having perhaps the better claim,
   Because it was grassy and wanted wear;
   Though as for that, the passing there
   Had worn them really about the same. ("The Road Not Taken")

   _____
   _____
   _____

2. The Heroism we recite
   Would be a normal thing
   Did not ourselves the Cubits warp
   For fear to be a King— ("We never know how high we are")

   _____
   _____
   _____

3. And when the Foreign Office find a Treaty's gone astray,
   Or the Admiralty lose some plans and drawings by the way,
   There may be a scrap of paper in the hall or on the stair—
   But it's useless to investigate—*Macavity's not there!* ("Macavity: The Mystery Cat")

   _____
   _____
   _____

4. All the world's a stage,
   And all the men and women merely players;
   They have their exits and their entrances;
   And one man in time plays many parts,
   His acts being seven ages. ("The Seven Ages of Man")

   _____
   _____
   _____

All-in-One Workbook
© Pearson Education, Inc. All rights reserved.

Name _____ Date _____

Poetry Collection: Robert Frost, Emily Dickinson, T. S. Eliot, and William Shakespeare
Vocabulary Builder

Word List

bafflement   depravity   disclosed   diverged
oblivion   rifled   treble   warp   woeful

A. DIRECTIONS: Match each word in Column A with the correct definition in Column B.

Column A
___ 1. diverged
___ 2. warp
___ 3. bafflement
___ 4. depravity
___ 5. woeful
___ 6. treble

Column B
A. sorrowful
B. corruption
C. high-pitched voice
D. puzzlement
E. twist
F. branched out

B. DIRECTIONS: In each of the following items, think about the meaning of the italicized word and then answer the question.

1. The burglars *rifled* through their victim's belongings. Would the burglars have searched thoroughly or rapidly?
_____

2. If someone *disclosed* a secret, would he or she keep it or not? Explain.
_____

3. Would being in a state of *oblivion* mean you are clearly aware of your surroundings? Explain.
_____

C. WORD STUDY: Use the context of the sentences and what you know about the Latin suffix *-ment* to explain your answer to each question.

1. If you experience *astonishment*, are you surprised or not?
_____

2. Is an *amendment* to a document a change to the document or a complete rewrite?
_____

3. Does a *postponement* mean that something will be done now or later?
_____

Name _____ Date _____

Poetry Collection: Robert Frost, Emily Dickinson, T. S. Eliot, and William Shakespeare
Conventions: Infinitives and Infinitive Phrases

An **infinitive** is a verb form preceded by the word *to* that acts as a noun, an adjective, or an adverb. An **infinitive phrase** is an infinitive with its modifiers or complements. Like infinitives, infinitive phrases can function as nouns, adjectives, or adverbs. Be careful not to mistake an infinitive or an infinitive phrase for a **prepositional phrase.** Whereas a prepositional phrase begins with *to* and ends with a noun or pronoun, an infinitive phrase always includes a verb.

Infinitive:	The schoolboy liked *to complain*. (acts as a noun, functioning as the direct object of the sentence)
Infinitive Phrase:	During the storm, I was afraid *to go outdoors*. (acts as an adverb by modifying *afraid*)
Prepositional Phrase:	We went *to the basement* when we heard the cat howling.

A. Directions: *On the line provided, write the infinitive phrase in each sentence. Be sure to write the entire infinitive phrase: the infinitive with all of its modifiers or complements. Then, identify whether the infinitive phrase functions as a noun, an adjective, or an adverb.*

1. We all wanted to find the cat.
   _____

2. My father said to look in the alley, but it wasn't there.
   _____

3. If I were a cat, I think the attic would be a perfect place to hide.
   _____

4. To escape capture was the cat's plan.
   _____

5. All of us were eager to recover our favorite pet.
   _____

B. Writing Application: *Write a brief paragraph describing one of your favorite hobbies. Use at least three infinitive phrases in your writing, and underline each infinitive phrase you use.*

_____
_____
_____
_____
_____
_____
_____

Name _____ Date _____

Poetry Collection: Robert Frost, Emily Dickinson, T. S. Eliot, and William Shakespeare
Support for Writing to Sources: Poem

Make prewriting notes for your poem by thinking about the issues below.

Rhyme Scheme:
_____
_____
_____
_____

Topic/Event/Experience/Emotion:
_____
_____
_____
_____
_____
_____

Images/Details/Phrases/Words:
_____
_____
_____
_____
_____
_____
_____

Name _____ Date _____

Poetry Collection: Robert Frost, Emily Dickinson, T. S. Eliot, and William Shakespeare

Support for Speaking and Listening: Panel Discussion

Use the following chart to take notes to prepare for your panel discussion on possible interpretations of each poem.

Title of Poem: _____

Possible Interpretations of Poem's Theme or Main Idea (Check the one you favor.)
1. _____ _____ Support in Text: _____ _____ _____ _____ 2. _____ _____ Support in Text: _____ _____ _____ _____ Panel's Position Statement: _____ _____

Name _____ Date _____

Poetry by Alice Walker, Bashō, Chiyojo, Walt Whitman, William Shakespeare

Writing About the Big Question

How does communication change us?

Big Question Vocabulary

aware	communication	comprehension	discuss	empathy
exchange	illuminate	informed	interpretation	meaning
react	relationship	resolution	respond	understanding

A. *Use one or more words from the list above to complete each sentence.*

1. Good _____ often helps deepen a(n) _____ between two people.

2. Kyra was _____ that she would have to improve her reading _____ skills if she were to score well on that test.

3. We workers attended the meeting to _____ our grievances, but the management seemed to _____ with hostility.

4. The professor's _____ of that story helped _____ the _____ for us.

B. *Follow the directions in responding to each of the items below.*

1. List two poems from this unit that have changed your perception of a person, place, event, or situation.
   _____
   _____

2. Write two sentences to explain how the poem changed your perception, and describe how this experience made you feel. Use at least two of the Big Question vocabulary words.
   _____
   _____

C. *Complete the sentence below. Then, write a short paragraph in which you connect the sentence to the Big Question.*

A powerful poem makes us **aware** of _____
_____
_____
_____

All-in-One Workbook

Name _____   Date _____

Poetry by Alice Walker, Bashō, Chiyojo, Walt Whitman, William Shakespeare

Literary Analysis: Lyric Poetry

Lyric poetry is poetry with a musical quality that expresses the thoughts and feelings of a single speaker. Unlike a narrative poem, a lyric does not try to tell a complete story. Instead, it describes an emotion or a mood, often by using vivid imagery, or language that appeals to the senses. A lyric poem is relatively short and usually achieves a single, unified effect.

There are a variety of lyric forms that can create different effects:

- A **sonnet** is a fourteen-line poem that is written in iambic pentameter and that rhymes. Two common sonnet types are the Italian, or Petrarchan, and the English, or Shakespearean. The English, or Shakespearean, sonnet consists of three quatrains, or four-line stanzas, and a final rhyming couplet.
- A **haiku** is an unrhymed Japanese verse form arranged into three lines of five, seven, and five syllables. A haiku often uses a striking image from nature to convey a strong emotion.
- A **free verse** poem does not follow a regular pattern. Free verse employs sound and rhythmic devices, such as alliteration and repetition, and may even use rhyme—but not in a regular pattern, as in metered poetry.

DIRECTIONS: *Analyze each poem. On the chart, write the type of lyric in the first column. Then, in the remaining columns, briefly describe the speaker of the poem, identify the speaker's emotion, and quote an example of a striking image or sound device.*

Author	Type of Lyric	Speaker	Emotion	Image/Sound Device
Walker				
Bashō				
Chiyojo				
Whitman				
Shakespeare				

Name _____ Date _____

Poetry by Alice Walker, Bashō, Chiyojo, Walt Whitman, William Shakespeare
Vocabulary Builder

Word List

    intermission   stout   wail   woes

A. Directions: *Revise each sentence so that the underlined vocabulary word is used logically. Be sure not to change the vocabulary word.*

1. Because she is stout of heart, she faces her future with great fear.
   _____

2. The film was 3 hours long with no intermission; we were grateful for the break.
   _____

3. He was cheerful as he recounted to us his many woes of the past year.
   _____

4. She sobbed with a wail of joy when she lost her ring.
   _____

B. Directions: *On the line, write the letter of the choice that is the best synonym, or word with a similar meaning, for each numbered word.*

___ 1. wail
    A. anger
    B. fear
    C. howl
    D. calm

___ 2. woes
    A. signals
    B. factories
    C. songs
    D. sorrows

___ 3. intermission
    A. analysis
    B. break
    C. communication
    D. alliance

___ 4. stout
    A. plentiful
    B. sturdy
    C. weary
    D. energetic

Name _____ Date _____

Poetry by Alice Walker, Bashō, Chiyojo, Walt Whitman, William Shakespeare
Support for Writing to Sources: Explanatory Text

Use a chart like the one shown to make prewriting notes for an essay comparing the relationship between lyric form and meaning in two poems from the selections.

Title of Poem 1: _____ **Lyric Form:** _____ **Characteristics of Form:** _____ _____ _____ **Relationship of Poem's Form to Its Meaning:** _____ _____ _____ _____	
Title of Poem 2: _____ **Lyric Form:** _____ **Characteristics of Form:** _____ _____ _____ **Relationship of Poem's Form to Its Meaning:** _____ _____ _____ _____	

Name _____ Date _____

Writing Process
Problem-and-Solution Essay

Prewriting: Narrowing Your Topic

To help focus your essay on a specific aspect of the problem, answer the questions in the following chart.

Question:	Your Answers:
What is the problem?	
Who is affected by the problem?	
What causes the problem to occur?	
What are some possible solutions to the problem?	

Drafting: Outlining the Problem

Use the following sunburst organizer to list aspects of the central problem. At the end of each ray, explore a detail or an aspect of the problem.

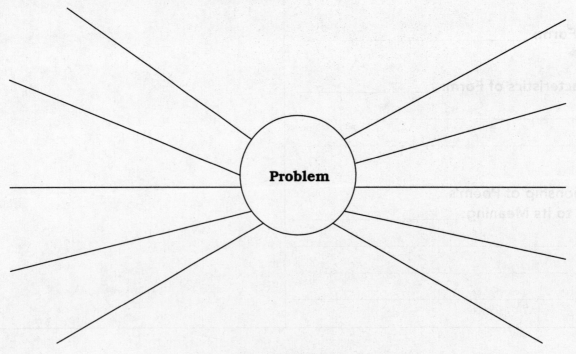

Name _____ Date _____

Writer's Toolbox

Conventions: Using Compound Structures to Combine Choppy Sentences

A series of short sentences can sound choppy and repetitious. To solve the problem, you can combine sentences by using words such as *and, but, or, either/or,* or *neither/nor* to form a compound structure.

Choppy	Compound Structure	Example
My brother Joe works hard in school. I work hard there, too.	Combined with Compound Subject	*My brother Joe and I* work hard in school.
I finished my homework. I studied for a math test.	Combined with Compound Verb	I *finished* my homework *and studied* for a math test.
I may study the textbook. I may study my class notes.	Combined with Compound Object	I may study *the textbook or my class notes.*
One of my favorite subjects is biology. The other is math.	Combined with Compound Predicate Nominative	My favorite subjects are *biology and math.*
The test was long. It was not very hard.	Combined with Compound Predicate Adjective	The test was *long but not very hard.*

Identifying Compound Structures

A. PRACTICE: On the line before each item, identify the compound structure that you would use to combine the pair of choppy sentences. The first one has been done as an example.

<u>compound verb</u>   1. Manuel does his homework in the evening. He also watches television.

_____   2. Sara attends a ballet class after school. Shawn attends the same ballet class.

_____   3. Leah plays basketball. She also plays softball.

_____   4. Performing drama is enjoyable. However, it is also difficult.

Using Compound Structures

B. WRITING APPLICATION: For each item, combine the two choppy sentences into a single sentence.

1. The swim team meets on Tuesdays. It also meets on Thursdays.
_____

2. The swim coach is strict. He is also fair.
_____

3. Todd belongs to the swim team. He also works as an after-school lifeguard.
_____

4. Simran may join the swim team. Simran may join the drama club.
_____

Name _____ Date _____

"**The Assassination of John F. Kennedy**" by Gwendolyn Brooks
"**Instead of an Elegy**" by G. S. Fraser
Vocabulary Builder

Selection Vocabulary

antic   delirium   requiem

A. DIRECTIONS: *Complete each sentence with a word, phrase, or clause that contains a context clue for the italicized word.*

1. The high fever brought on a period of *delirium*, in which the patient experienced _____.

2. The frisky puppy nipped me with his teeth, but I knew it was an *antic* gesture because _____.

3. At the cathedral yesterday there was a *requiem* because _____.

Academic Vocabulary

resolution   counteract   implicit

B. DIRECTIONS: *Write a sentence to follow each direction. Make sure to use the word in italics at least once in your response.*

1. Name a problem and an effective *resolution*.
   _____

2. If a person accidentally becomes sunburned, how might he or she *counteract* the pain?
   _____

3. An actor suddenly stops in the middle of a line and looks around helplessly. Describe the *implicit* message such actions convey.
   _____

Name _____ Date _____

"The Assassination of John F. Kennedy" by Gwendolyn Brooks
"Instead of an Elegy" by G. S. Fraser
Take Notes for Discussion

Before the Group Discussion: Read the following passage.

> Bullets blot out the Life-Time-smile,
> Apollo of the picture-page,
> Blunt-faced young lion
> Caught by vile
> Death in an everlasting cage:

During the Discussion: As your group discusses each question, take notes on how other students' ideas either differ from or build upon your own.

Discussion Questions	Other Ideas Expressed	Comparison to My Own Ideas
1. What literary techniques does the poet use in this stanza? Are they effective? Why or why not?		
2. What overall impression of Kennedy does the speaker communicate?		

Name _____ Date _____

"The Assassination of John F. Kennedy" by Gwendolyn Brooks
"Instead of an Elegy" by G. S. Fraser
Take Notes for Writing to Sources

Planning Your Expository Text: Before you begin drafting your **expository essay,** use the chart below to organize your ideas. The first column lists the two poems and poets. In the second and third columns, jot down notes about how each poet communicates a sense of grief for Kennedy as a private person and as a public figure. Be sure to include notes about each poet's use of literary techniques, word choice, and poetic structure.

Poet	Grief for Kennedy as a Private Person	Grief for Kennedy as a Public Figure
Gwendolyn Brooks: "The Assassination of John F. Kennedy"		
G. S. Fraser: "Instead of an Elegy"		

Name _____ Date _____

"The Assassination of John F. Kennedy" by Gwendolyn Brooks
"Instead of an Elegy" by G. S. Fraser

Take Notes for Research

As you research the **world's reactions to the assassination of President Kennedy,** use the forms below to take notes from your sources. As necessary, continue your notes on the back of this page, on note cards, or in a word-processing document.

Source Information   Check one: ☐ Primary Source   ☐ Secondary Source

Title: _____   Author: _____

Publication Information: _____

Page(s): _____

Main Idea: _____

Quotation or Paraphrase: _____

Source Information   Check one: ☐ Primary Source   ☐ Secondary Source

Title: _____   Author: _____

Publication Information: _____

Page(s): _____

Main Idea: _____

Quotation or Paraphrase: _____

Source Information   Check one: ☐ Primary Source   ☐ Secondary Source

Title: _____   Author: _____

Publication Information: _____

Page(s): _____

Main Idea: _____

Quotation or Paraphrase: _____

Name _____ Date _____

from *A White House Diary,* by Lady Bird Johnson
Vocabulary Builder

Selection Vocabulary

confines   immaculate   poignant

A. DIRECTIONS: *Decide whether each statement below is true or false. On the line before each item, write TRUE or FALSE. Then explain your answers.*

_____ 1. The *confines* of a closet are too cramped to serve as an office for two people.
_____

_____ 2. A soft-drink advertisement is a good example of a *poignant* sight.
_____

_____ 3. If a room is *immaculate*, it needs a good cleaning.
_____

Academic Vocabulary

advocate   conduct   intimate

B. DIRECTIONS: *Write a response to each question. Make sure to use the word in italics at least once in your response.*

1. Which is a more *intimate* source of information—a letter or a newspaper article? Explain.
_____
_____

2. How might a president's *conduct* differ as a public figure in his office and as a father at home with his family?
_____
_____

3. Why might such organizations as the American Red Cross ask popular figures to *advocate* for them?
_____
_____

Name _____ Date _____

from A White House Diary, by Lady Bird Johnson
Take Notes for Discussion

Before the Partner Discussion: Read the following passage from the selection.

> The flight to Washington was silent, each sitting with his own thoughts. One of mine was a recollection of what I had said about Lyndon a long time ago—he's a good man in a tight spot. I remembered one little thing he had said in that hospital room—"Tell the children to get a Secret Service man with them."

During the Discussion: As you discuss each question, take notes on how your partner's ideas either differ from or build upon your own.

Discussion Questions	Other Ideas Expressed	Comparison to My Own Ideas
1. What does it mean to be "in a tight spot"? How do President Johnson's actions demonstrate that he is "a good man" in such a situation?		
2. What does this recollection suggest about Mrs. Johnson's role and conduct as a political wife?		

All-in-One Workbook

Name _____ Date _____

from A White House Diary, by Lady Bird Johnson
Take Notes for Research

Begin your research on the causes supported by a particular first lady by writing the name of the one you have chosen at the top of the chart below. Then use the chart to take notes from your sources. As necessary, continue your notes on the back of this page, on note cards, or in a word-processing document.

First Lady: _____

Main Idea _____ _____ **Quotation or Paraphrase** _____ _____ _____ _____ _____ **Source Information** _____ _____ _____ _____ _____	**Main Idea** _____ _____ **Quotation or Paraphrase** _____ _____ _____ _____ _____ **Source Information** _____ _____ _____ _____ _____
Main Idea _____ _____ **Quotation or Paraphrase** _____ _____ _____ _____ _____ **Source Information** _____ _____ _____ _____ _____	**Main Idea** _____ _____ **Quotation or Paraphrase** _____ _____ _____ _____ _____ **Source Information** _____ _____ _____ _____ _____

Name _____ Date _____

from A White House Diary, by Lady Bird Johnson
Take Notes for Writing to Sources

Planning Your Argument: Before you begin drafting your character analysis, use the chart below to organize your ideas. Follow the directions at the top of each box.

---

1. Reread the diary entry, and jot down notes about the details that reveal Mrs. Johnson's character. Use the following cues to help you.

Details from her observations: _____
_____
_____
_____

Details from her actions and reactions: _____
_____
_____
_____
_____

Details from her words (use direct quotations when possible): _____
_____
_____
_____
_____

---

2. Based on your notes, develop a central claim. What type of person do you think Mrs. Johnson was?
_____
_____
_____
_____
_____
_____
_____

As you draft your character analysis, begin with your central claim. Then, in the body of the analysis, use the details that you gathered to support your central claim. Finally, write a conclusion in which you sum up your assertions about Mrs. Johnson and restate your central claim in strong, direct language.

All-in-One Workbook
© Pearson Education, Inc. All rights reserved.

Name _____   Date _____

"American History" by Judith Ortiz Cofer
Vocabulary Builder

Selection Vocabulary

    dilapidated   profound   vigilant

A. DIRECTIONS: *Revise each sentence so that the italicized vocabulary word is used logically. Be sure not to change the vocabulary word.*

1. His sadness was *profound* when he learned that he had won the election.
   _____

2. It is rarely necessary for a person to be *vigilant* when crossing a busy downtown street.
   _____

3. The royal family was delighted to find the family lodge in such a *dilapidated* condition.
   _____

Academic Vocabulary

    disseminating   forum   pose

B. DIRECTIONS: *Write the letter of the word or phrase that is the best synonym for the italicized word. Then use the italicized word in a complete sentence.*

_____ 1. *disseminating*
      A. preserving   C. rewording
      B. spreading   D. refuting
_____

_____ 2. *forum*
      A. a space for discussion   C. a restaurant for dining
      B. a park for playing   D. a library for studying
_____

_____ 3. *pose*
      A. suggest   C. cite
      B. respond   D. contrast
_____

All-in-One Workbook
© Pearson Education, Inc. All rights reserved.

Name _____ Date _____

"American History" by Judith Ortiz Cofer
Take Notes for Discussion

Before the One-on-One Discussion: Read the following passage from the selection.

> I would hear them talking softly in the kitchen for hours that night. They would not discuss their dreams for the future, or life in Puerto Rico, as they often did; that night they would talk sadly about the young widow and her two children, as if they were family. For the next few days, we would observe *luto* in our apartment; that is, we would practice restraint and silence—no loud music or laughter. Some of the women of El Building would wear black for weeks.

During the Discussion: As you discuss each question, take notes on how your partner's ideas either differ from or build upon your own.

Discussion Questions	Other Ideas Expressed	Comparison to My Own Ideas
1. What does this passage reveal about the effect of the president's death on people in Elena's community?		
2. Based on this passage, what can you infer about the reactions most Americans had to the assassination?		

All-in-One Workbook
© Pearson Education, Inc. All rights reserved.

Name _____ Date _____

"American History" by Judith Ortiz Cofer
Take Notes for Research

As you research **the role the media played in spreading the news of President Kennedy's death,** you can use the organizer below to take notes from your sources. As necessary, continue your notes on the back of this page, on note cards, or in a word-processing document.

The Role of the Media	
Main Idea _____ **Quotation or Paraphrase** _____ _____ _____ _____ _____ **Source Information** _____ _____ _____ _____ _____	**Main Idea** _____ **Quotation or Paraphrase** _____ _____ _____ _____ _____ **Source Information** _____ _____ _____ _____ _____
Main Idea _____ **Quotation or Paraphrase** _____ _____ _____ _____ _____ **Source Information** _____ _____ _____ _____ _____	**Main Idea** _____ **Quotation or Paraphrase** _____ _____ _____ _____ _____ **Source Information** _____ _____ _____ _____ _____

All-in-One Workbook
© Pearson Education, Inc. All rights reserved.

Name _____ Date _____

"American History" by Judith Ortiz Cofer
Take Notes for Writing to Sources

Planning Your Analysis: Before you begin drafting your **analytical essay,** use the chart below to organize your ideas. In the second column of the chart, record Elena's observations about the two realms of feelings. Jot down details and direct quotations from the text as well as your own insights and ideas.

Points of Comparison	Elena's Observations and My Insights
1. The feelings of connection Elena has for her neighbors next door	
2. The feelings of connection her family and neighbors have for the Kennedy family	

All-in-One Workbook
© Pearson Education, Inc. All rights reserved.

Address Before a Joint Session of the Congress, November 27, 1963
by Lyndon Baines Johnson
Vocabulary Builder

Selection Vocabulary
eulogy   formidable   fortitude

A. *Decide whether each statement below is true or false. On the line before each item, write TRUE or FALSE. Then explain your answers.*

_____ 1. People with *fortitude* need to build up their strength.
_____

_____ 2. A kitten is a *formidable* animal.
_____

_____ 3. A *eulogy* is a speech that is most often given during a graduation ceremony.
_____

Academic Vocabulary
articulated   concise   stirs

B. DIRECTIONS: *Provide an explanation for your answer to each question.*

1. What type of story often <u>stirs</u> people's emotions?
_____
_____

2. Would a lengthy speech be considered *concise*?
_____

3. In a diary entry and in a speech, Lady Bird Johnson and Lyndon Johnson *articulated* their feelings about the death of John F. Kennedy. Whose feelings do you think are *articulated* more memorably? Explain.
_____
_____
_____

All-in-One Workbook
© Pearson Education, Inc. All rights reserved.

Name _____ Date _____

Address Before a Joint Session of the Congress, November 27, 1963
by Lyndon Baines Johnson
Take Notes for Discussion

Before the Partner Discussion: Read the following passage from the selection. Then, fill out the chart below with ideas you would like to discuss and examples from the text that support your ideas.

> John Kennedy's death commands what his life conveyed—that America must move forward. The time has come for Americans of all races and creeds and political beliefs to understand and to respect one another. So let us put an end to the teaching and the preaching of hate and evil and violence.

Discussion Questions	My Ideas	Examples From the Text
1. What lesson does Johnson take from Kennedy's death?		
2. Is President Johnson's response to the Kennedy assassination appropriate? Why or why not?		

During the Discussion: As you discuss each question, take notes on how your partner's ideas either differ from or build upon your own.

Discussion Questions	Other Ideas Expressed	Comparison to My Own Ideas
1. What lesson does Johnson take from Kennedy's death?		
2. Is President Johnson's response to the Kennedy assassination appropriate? Why or why not?		

All-in-One Workbook
© Pearson Education, Inc. All rights reserved.

Name _____ Date _____

Address Before a Joint Session of the Congress, November 27, 1963
by Lyndon Baines Johnson

Take Notes for Research

As you research a **speech given by President Kennedy or President Johnson,** you can use the organizer below to take notes from your sources. At the top, identify the president you have chosen as your research topic and the title and date of the speech. As necessary, continue your notes on the back of this page, on note cards, or in a word-processing document.

President _____ **Speech Title** _____ **Date** _____	
Main Idea _____ _____ Quotation or Paraphrase _____ _____ _____ _____ _____ Source Information _____ _____ _____ _____ _____	Main Idea _____ _____ Quotation or Paraphrase _____ _____ _____ _____ _____ Source Information _____ _____ _____ _____ _____
Main Idea _____ _____ Quotation or Paraphrase _____ _____ _____ _____ _____ Source Information _____ _____ _____ _____ _____	Main Idea _____ _____ Quotation or Paraphrase _____ _____ _____ _____ _____ Source Information _____ _____ _____ _____ _____

All-in-One Workbook
© Pearson Education, Inc. All rights reserved.

Name _____   Date _____

Address Before a Joint Session of the Congress, November 27, 1963
by Lyndon Baines Johnson
Take Notes for Writing to Sources

Planning Your Narrative: Before you begin drafting your **historical narrative,** use the chart below to organize your ideas. Follow the directions in each box.

---

1. Describe your character.

Age: _____   Appearance: _____

Occupation: _____

Personality traits: _____
_____

How he or she was affected by President Kennedy's death: _____
_____
_____

---

2. Outline the plot. Create a conflict that the character faces. Jot down details related to the assassination and Johnson's speech.

_____
_____
_____
_____
_____
_____
_____
_____
_____

---

3. Plan the resolution. Jot down notes regarding how the conflict is solved.

_____
_____
_____
_____
_____
_____
_____
_____

All-in-One Workbook
© Pearson Education, Inc. All rights reserved.

Name _____ Date _____

Images of a Tragedy
Vocabulary Builder and Take Notes for Writing to Sources

Academic Vocabulary

    caption   consider   crystallize

DIRECTIONS: Complete each sentence with a word, phrase, or clause that contains a context clue for the underlined word.

1. In the photo, it was difficult to see the figures standing in the fog. However, the <u>caption</u> _____ .

2. If you <u>consider</u> what the photographer intended, you _____ _____ .

3. Often, photographs are able to <u>crystallize</u> such concepts as joy or grief by _____ _____ .

Take Notes for Writing to Sources

Planning Your Article: Before you begin drafting your **magazine article,** use the chart below to organize your ideas. Follow the directions at the top of each box.

Image	Details
1. Identify the topic of each image in the sequence.	**2.** Next to each topic, jot down what you will write about the image. Keep your audience in mind, remembering that you are to assume that they do not know about these events.

All-in-One Workbook
© Pearson Education, Inc. All rights reserved.

Name _____ Date _____

Unit 4: Drama
Big Question Vocabulary—1

The Big Question: Do our differences define us?

When someone is new to a group, it is important to help him or her feel welcome and to understand that, even though people may act differently because of different experiences and culture, they normally experience the same feelings that you do.

accept: to regard as normal, suitable, or usual

defend: to support someone or something that is being hurt or criticized

differentiate: to recognize the differences between two or more things

discriminate: to treat someone differently and/or unfairly

understanding: knowledge that is based on understanding or experience

DIRECTIONS: *Use all the vocabulary words to fill in the callouts.*

Caroline said, "That new girl, Nubia, is really weird. She speaks funny and her clothing is so colorful and loose! I don't want her to sit with us at lunch anymore!"

Caroline's lunch buddies did not agree. They thought it was important to welcome Nubia as a newcomer to their community. They said the following in response to Caroline:

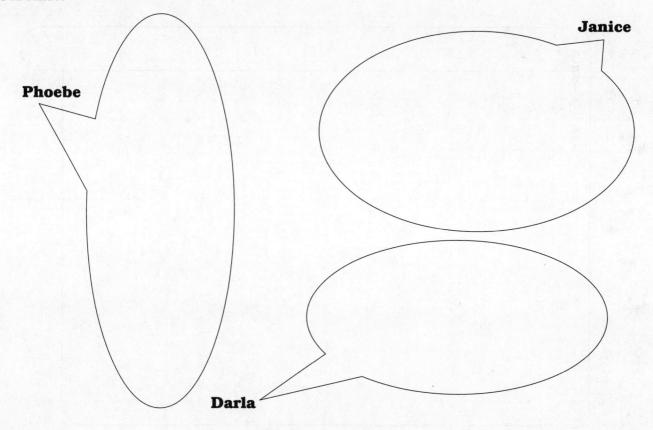

Unit 4: Drama
Big Question Vocabulary—2

The Big Question: Do our differences define us?

When you are in your own culture, you are similar to those around you, but if you take a trip to a foreign place you will quickly discover that you are suddenly the "different" one.

background: a person's family history, education, and social class

culture: ideas, beliefs, and customs that are shared by people in a society

determine: to conclude or ascertain after reasoning, observation, study, and so on

unique: having no like or equal; incomparable

values: one's principles concerning right and wrong and what is important in life

DIRECTIONS: *Use all the vocabulary words to complete the following exercise.*

You have just landed in a new country. Everybody is looking at you strangely. You are dressed differently from them, and your words sound like gibberish to them. There is only one person who speaks English, and he will be there for only twenty-four hours. He has offered to translate a short document that you write to introduce yourself and your culture to the people who live here.

Name _____ Date _____

Unit 4: Drama
Big Question Vocabulary—3

The Big Question: Do our differences define us?

Discrimination is often a result of people not having enough knowledge about others who appear different. Open dialogue can usually help people understand one another and can help people build tolerance and mutual respect.

assimilated: absorbed into the main cultural group

conformity: behavior that is within the accepted rules of a society or a group and is the same as that of most other people

differences: the quality or condition of being unlike or dissimilar

individuality: characteristics or qualities that distinguish one person from other people

similarity: having a likeness or a resemblance to something else or someone else

DIRECTIONS: *Newcomers to your school are feeling excluded. Write a proposed set of guidelines that tell your fellow students how newcomers should be treated at school. Use all of the vocabulary words.*

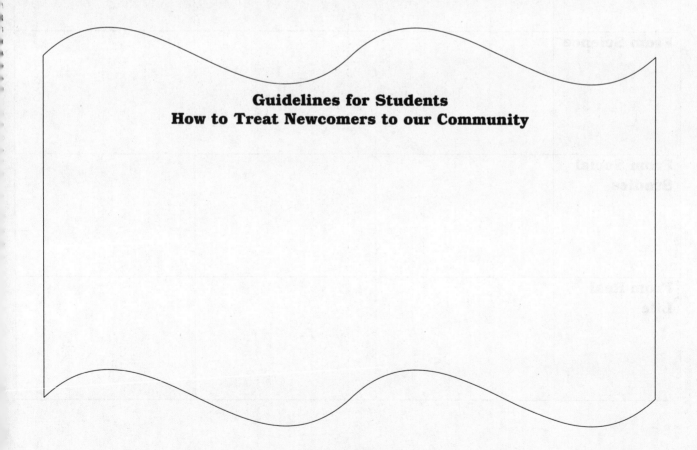

**Guidelines for Students
How to Treat Newcomers to our Community**

Name _____ Date _____

Unit 4: Drama
Applying the Big Question

The Big Question: Do our differences define us?

DIRECTIONS: Complete the chart below to apply what you have learned about differences. One row has been completed for you.

Example	Kinds of differences	The effect of the differences	What I Learned
From Literature	Differences in authority and position in "The Inspector-General"	The peasant outsmarts the powerful inspector-general.	Differences in authority and position don't define how clever someone is.
From Literature			
From Science			
From Social Studies			
From Real Life			

Name _____ Date _____

The Tragedy of Romeo and Juliet, Act I, by William Shakespeare
Writing About the Big Question

Do our differences define us?

Big Question Vocabulary

accept	assimilated	background	conformity	culture
defend	determine	differences	differentiate	discriminate
individuality	similarity	understanding	unique	values

A. *Use one or more words from the list above to complete each sentence.*

1. The Big Question asks if our _____ define us.

2. Your _____ plays a role in making you who you are.

3. America has _____ people of many nations.

4. Although immigrants become part of the American way of life, many still cling to important aspects of their _____.

B. *Follow the directions in responding to each of the items below.*

1. In two sentences, name two ways that immigrant groups living in the United States might differ.
   _____
   _____

2. Write two sentences describing how one of the differences you named is a positive thing. Use at least two of the Big Question vocabulary words.
   _____
   _____

C. *In* The Tragedy of Romeo and Juliet, *two young lovers come from families locked in a deadly feud. That difference defines their relationship and forces the plot toward tragic consequences. Complete the sentence below. Then, write a short paragraph in which you connect this idea to the Big Question.*

When family **differences** stand between lovers, they must _____
or _____
_____
_____
_____

All-in-One Workbook
© Pearson Education, Inc. All rights reserved.

Name _____ Date _____

The Tragedy of Romeo and Juliet, Act I, by William Shakespeare
Literary Analysis: Dialogue and Stage Directions

Dialogue is conversation between or among characters. In prose, dialogue is usually set off with quotation marks. In drama, the dialogue generally follows the name of the speaker, as in this example:

> **BENVOLIO.** I aimed so near when I supposed you loved.
> **ROMEO.** A right good markman. And she's fair I love.

Dialogue reveals the personalities and relationships of the characters and advances the action of a play.

Stage directions are notes in the text of a play that describe how the work should be performed, or staged. These instructions are usually printed in italics and sometimes set in brackets or parentheses. They describe scenes, lighting, sound effects, and the appearance and physical actions of the characters, as in this example:

> **Scene iii.** FRIAR LAWRENCE's cell.
> [*Enter.* FRIAR LAWRENCE *alone, with a basket.*]

As you read, notice how the dialogue and stage directions work together to help you "see" and "hear" the play in your mind.

DIRECTIONS: *Read this passage from Act I and then use the lines below to answer the questions.*

> NURSE. Madam, your mother craves a word with you.
> ROMEO. What is her mother?
> NURSE. Marry, bachelor,
>   Her mother is the lady of the house,
>   And a good lady, and a wise and virtuous.
>   I nursed her daughter that you talked withal.
>   I tell you, he that can lay hold of her
>   Shall have the chinks.
> ROMEO. *(aside)* Is she a Capulet?
>   O dear account! My life is my foe's dark debt. (Act I, Scene v, ll. 111–117)

1. In the context of the scene, what does this dialogue reveal?
   _____

2. What do the lines reveal about Nurse's and Juliet's relationship?
   _____
   _____
   _____

3. What do the lines foreshadow for the plot of the play?
   _____
   _____
   _____

Name _____ Date _____

The Tragedy of Romeo and Juliet, Act I, by William Shakespeare
Reading: Summarize

Summarizing is briefly stating the main points in a piece of writing. Stopping periodically to summarize what you have read helps you to check your comprehension before you read further.

To be sure that you understand Shakespeare's language before you summarize long passages, use the glosses—the numbered explanations that appear alongside the text.

- If you are confused by a passage, check to see if there is a gloss and read the corresponding explanation.
- Reread the passage, using the information from the gloss to be sure you grasp the meaning of the passage.

DIRECTIONS: *Use the glosses to help you answer the following questions about what you read in Act I of the play.*

1. In your own words, summarize what is happening in Verona based on lines 1–4 of the Prologue.

   _____
   _____
   _____

2. In Scene i, as the two Montague Servingmen approach the two Capulet Servingmen, Sampson says, "Let us take the law of our sides; let them begin." What does he mean?

   _____
   _____

3. Later in Scene i, Benvolio and Montague talk about how unhappy Romeo has been. Then, they see Romeo. Benvolio tells Montague to leave so that he can talk to Romeo alone. Montague says, "I would thou wert so happy by thy stay / To hear true shrift." Put this wish into your own words.

   _____
   _____

4. In Scene iii, Juliet's mother tells her to "Read o'er the volume of young Paris's face." Refer to that passage (lines 81–92) and, with the help of glosses 9 and 10, summarize the advice Lady Capulet gives to her daughter.

   _____
   _____
   _____
   _____

All-in-One Workbook
© Pearson Education, Inc. All rights reserved.

Name _____ Date _____

The Tragedy of Romeo and Juliet, Act I, by William Shakespeare
Vocabulary Builder

Word List

adversary   augmenting   grievance   oppression   pernicious   transgression

A. DIRECTIONS: *In each of the following items, think about the meaning of the italicized word and then answer the question.*

1. Would you be likely to praise an action that had *pernicious* consequences? Why or why not?
   _____

2. Would a person expressing a *grievance* be likely to seem happy or sad? Explain.
   _____

3. If your employer announces that she is *augmenting* your salary, how would you feel?
   _____

4. Would you go out of your way to help an *adversary*? Explain.
   _____
   _____

5. Would a person experiencing *oppression* feel free or burdened? Explain.
   _____
   _____

6. Would someone committing a *transgression* be doing the right thing?
   _____

B. WORD STUDY: The prefix *trans-* means "across" or "through." Answer each of the following questions using one of these words containing *trans-*: *transgression, transition, transitory, translucent, transport.*

1. What is one item that is *translucent*?
   _____

2. What is one *transition* that people often make in life?
   _____

3. What are two ways to *transport* goods?
   _____

4. What kind of treatment does someone who has committed a *transgression* deserve?
   _____

5. How would you feel if you found out that your troubles are *transitory*?
   _____

All-in-One Workbook
© Pearson Education, Inc. All rights reserved.

Name _____ Date _____

The Tragedy of Romeo and Juliet, Act II, by William Shakespeare
Writing About the Big Question

Do our differences define us?

Big Question Vocabulary

accept	assimilated	background	conformity	culture
defend	determine	differences	differentiate	discriminate
individuality	similarity	understanding	unique	values

A. *Use one or more words from the list above to complete each sentence.*

1. My friend Steve wears _____ outfits to school, like bright orange shirts paired with purple pants.

2. He is quick to _____ his clothing by saying that he dresses to suit his mood.

3. You can certainly _____ between him and all the other boys in our class.

4. I have to admit that I admire his _____.

B. *Follow the directions in responding to each of the items below.*

1. In two sentences, describe a time when you stood out from others in your school.
   _____
   _____

2. Write two sentences explaining what the above experience revealed about you. Use at least two of the Big Question vocabulary words.
   _____
   _____

C. *In* The Tragedy of Romeo and Juliet, *two young lovers come from families locked in a deadly feud. That difference defines their relationship and forces the plot toward tragic consequences. Complete the sentence below. Then, write a short paragraph in which you connect this idea to the Big Question.*

It is important to embrace our differences because _____
_____
_____
_____
_____

The Tragedy of Romeo and Juliet, Act II, by William Shakespeare
Literary Analysis: Blank Verse

Blank verse is unrhymed poetry written in a meter called iambic pentameter. A line written in iambic pentameter includes five stressed syllables, each preceded by an unstressed syllable, as in the following example:

'Tĭs bút thў náme thăt ís mў énemў.

Thŏu árt thўsélf thŏugh nót ă Móntăgué.

Much of *The Tragedy of Romeo and Juliet* is written in blank verse. Shakespeare uses its formal meter to reinforce character rank. Important or aristocratic characters typically speak in blank verse. Minor or comic characters often do not speak in verse.

DIRECTIONS: *Mark the stressed and unstressed syllables in these lines from Act II, Scene v. Put a check mark next to any line that has one extra syllable or any line not written in iambic pentameter. The first line has been marked for you.*

JULIET. Thĕ clóck strŭck níne whĕn Í dĭd sénd thĕ núrse;
In half an hour she promised to return.
Perchance she cannot meet him. That's not so.
O, she is lame! Love's heralds should be thoughts,
5 Which ten times faster glide than the sun's beams
Driving back shadows over low'ring hills.
Therefore do nimble-pinioned doves draw Love,
And therefore hath the wind-swift Cupid wings.
Now is the sun upon the highmost hill
10 Of this day's journey, and from nine till twelve
Is three long hours, yet she is not come.
Had she affections and warm youthful blood,
She would be as swift in motion as a ball;
My words would bandy her to my sweet love,
15 And his to me.
But old folks, many feign as they were dead—
Unwieldy, slow, heavy and pale as lead.

Name _____ Date _____

The Tragedy of Romeo and Juliet, Act II, by William Shakespeare
Reading: Read in Sentences

When reading a play that has long passages of blank verse, **read in sentences,** just as if you were reading a poem. Pause according to punctuation and not necessarily at the end of each line. Reading in this way will help clarify the meaning of each sentence.

Once you have grasped the meanings of individual sentences in blank verse, you can more easily and more accurately understand and summarize long passages.

DIRECTIONS: *Read the following passage, and then answer the items on the lines provided.*

1 Two of the fairest stars in all the heaven,
2 Having some business, do entreat her eyes
3 To twinkle in their spheres till they return.
4 What if her eyes were there, they in her head?
5 The brightness of her cheek would shame those stars
6 As daylight doth a lamp; her eyes in heaven
7 Would through the airy region stream so bright
8 That birds would sing and think it were not night.

1. At the end of which line(s) should you make no pause at all?
   _____

2. At the end of which line(s) should you make a major pause?
   _____

3. At the end of which line(s) should you make a minor pause?
   _____

4. Write a brief summary of the main points in this passage.
   _____
   _____
   _____
   _____
   _____

Name _____ Date _____

The Tragedy of Romeo and Juliet, Act II, by William Shakespeare
Vocabulary Builder

Word List

intercession   lamentable   predominan   procure   sallow   unwieldly

A. DIRECTIONS: *For each of the following items, think about the meaning of the italicized word and then answer the question.*

1. Would an *unwieldy* burden be easy or difficult to carry? Why?
   _____

2. If you received *lamentable* news, how would you feel?
   _____

3. Is *intercession* typically something you undertake on your own behalf or for the sake of someone else?
   _____

4. If a species of tree is *predominant* in your neighborhood, are there many or few of that species?
   _____

5. What might cause a person with a normally rosy complexion to suddenly look *sallow*?
   _____

6. If you *procure* something, does that usually mean you throw it away? Explain.
   _____

B. WORD STUDY: The Latin prefix *pro-* means "before," "forth," or "forward." Answer each of the following questions using one of these words containing *pro-*: procure, profound, profuse, protrude, provoke.

1. What would be difficult to *procure* in the desert?
   _____

2. What can you do to fix teeth that *protrude*?
   _____

3. How might someone react if you *provoke* that person?
   _____

4. What might be the subject of a *profound* discussion?
   _____

5. If a critic is *profuse* in her praise of a movie, how well did she like the movie?
   _____

Name _____ Date _____

The Tragedy of Romeo and Juliet, Act III, by William Shakespeare
Writing About the Big Question

Do our differences define us?

Big Question Vocabulary

accept	assimilated	background	conformity	culture
defend	determine	differences	differentiate	discriminate
individuality	similarity	understanding	unique	values

A. *Use one or more words from the list above to complete each sentence.*

1. Rosa Parks did not think that others should _____ against her because of her race.

2. In the South in 1955, there was an _____ that African Americans sit in a section in the back of the bus.

3. Parks refused to _____ this practice.

4. Her act of defiance helped _____ the course of the civil rights movement in America.

B. *Follow the directions in responding to each of the items below.*

1. In two sentences, tell why you think people are discriminated against because they are different. Use at least two of the Big Question vocabulary words.

   _____
   _____

2. Write two sentences explaining two things you might do to fight discrimination.

   _____
   _____

C. *In* The Tragedy of Romeo and Juliet, *two young lovers come from families locked in a deadly feud. That difference defines their relationship and forces the plot toward tragic consequences. Complete the sentence below. Then, write a short paragraph in which you connect this idea to the Big Question.*

Family differences are especially hard to overcome because _____
_____
_____
_____
_____

All-in-One Workbook

The Tragedy of Romeo and Juliet, Act III, by William Shakespeare
Literary Analysis: Dramatic Speeches

Characters in plays often deliver these types of **dramatic speeches:**

- **Soliloquy:** a lengthy speech in which a character—usually alone on stage—expresses his or her true thoughts or feelings. Soliloquies are unheard by other characters.
- **Aside:** a brief remark by a character revealing his or her true thoughts or feelings, unheard by other characters.
- **Monologue:** a lengthy speech by one person. Unlike a soliloquy, a monologue is addressed to other characters.

Characters often add meaning to speeches by making **allusions**—references to well-known people, places, or events from mythology or literature. For example, in Act II, Mercutio insultingly calls Tybalt "Prince of Cats," alluding to a cat named Tybalt in French fables.

DIRECTIONS: *Answer the questions that follow about an aside, a soliloquy, a monologue, and an allusion.*

1. In Scene v, Juliet's mother refers to Romeo as a villain. In an aside, Juliet says, "Villain and he be many miles asunder." What is the effect of this aside? Why do you think Shakespeare wrote just the one remark as an aside?

   _____

2. In Scene v, Capulet delivers a monologue when he discovers that Juliet has rejected the match with Paris. Reread lines 177–197. What makes this speech a monologue?

   _____
   _____

3. Why is it important for Juliet and the others to hear Capulet's monologue?

   _____

4. At the close of Scene v, Juliet delivers a soliloquy. Reread lines 237–244. What makes these last eight lines a soliloquy?

   _____
   _____

5. Explain Juliet's allusion to Greek mythology in the opening lines of Scene ii.
   Gallop apace, you fiery-footed steeds,
   Toward Phoebus' lodging!

   _____
   _____

Name _____ Date _____

The Tragedy of Romeo and Juliet, Act III, by William Shakespeare
Reading: Paraphrase

When you read a long passage in a Shakespearean play, you will often find it helpful to **paraphrase** it, or restate the lines in your own words. For example, compare these two versions of a speech by Romeo:

Shakespeare's version: This gentleman, the prince's near ally, / My very friend, hath got his mortal hurt / In my behalf.

Paraphrase: My good friend, a close relative of the prince, has been fatally wounded in defending me.

Once you have paraphrased small portions of text, you can more easily and accurately understand and summarize the entire passage.

DIRECTIONS: *Paraphrase the following passages from Act III. Remember that a paraphrase is a restatement in your own words for clarity. It is not a summary.*

1. **TYBALT.** Romeo, the love I bear thee can afford
   No better term than this: thou art a villain. (Scene i, ll. 57–58)
   _____
   _____

2. **PRINCE.** My blood for your rude brawls doth lie a-bleeding;
   But I'll amerce you with so strong a fine
   That you shall all repent the loss of mine. (Scene i, ll. 188–190)
   _____
   _____

3. **JULIET.** So tedious is this day
   As is the night before some festival
   To an impatient child that hath new robes
   And may not wear them. (Scene ii, ll. 28–31)
   _____
   _____
   _____

Name _____ Date _____

The Tragedy of Romeo and Juliet, Act III, by William Shakespeare
Vocabulary Builder

Word List

eloquence   exile   fickle   fray   gallant   martial

A. DIRECTIONS: *For each of the following items, think about the meaning of the italicized word and then answer the question.*

1. Would you describe the people participating on both sides of a *fray* as hostile or friendly? Explain.
   _____

2. Can a romance in which one or both partners are *fickle* be described as stable and happy? Why or why not?
   _____

3. Would the sound of *martial* music evoke war or peace? Explain.
   _____

4. If you call someone *gallant*, is that a compliment or an insult? Explain.
   _____

5. Would a ruler most likely *exile* someone for good deeds or bad ones? Explain.
   _____

6. Would speaking with *eloquence* probably keep an audience interested? Why or why not?
   _____

B. WORD STUDY: The Latin root *-loque-* means "to speak." Answer each of the following questions using one of these words containing *-loque-*: *colloquial, eloquence, loquacious, soliloquy, ventriloquist.*

1. Who gives a *soliloquy*?
   _____

2. With whom does a *ventriloquist* usually converse?
   _____

3. What is an example of when it is appropriate to use *colloquial* language?
   _____

4. What difficulty might you have conversing with someone who is *loquacious*?
   _____

5. How might you be affected by the *eloquence* of a speech?
   _____

Name _____ Date _____

The Tragedy of Romeo and Juliet, Act IV, by William Shakespeare
Writing About the Big Question

Do our differences define us?

Big Question Vocabulary

accept	assimilated	background	conformity	culture
defend	determine	differences	differentiate	discriminate
individuality	similarity	understanding	unique	values

A. *Use one or more words from the list above to complete each sentence.*

1. Some people believe that extreme _____ prevents original thought.

2. Galileo was an original thinker with a great _____ of science.

3. He got into trouble when he dared to _____ the idea that the earth revolved around the sun.

4. The religious _____ of the time held fast to the idea that the earth was the center of the universe.

B. *Follow the directions in responding to each of the items below.*

1. In two sentences, describe a time when your thinking did not conform with the thinking of your classmates.
   _____
   _____

2. Write two sentences defending your preceding position. Use at least two of the Big Question vocabulary words.
   _____
   _____

C. *In* The Tragedy of Romeo and Juliet, *two young lovers come from families locked in a deadly feud. That difference defines their relationship and forces the plot toward tragic consequences. Complete the sentence below. Then, write a short paragraph in which you connect this idea to the Big Question.*

Differences between families can result in tragedy if _____
_____
_____
_____
_____

Name _____ Date _____

The Tragedy of Romeo and Juliet, Act IV, by William Shakespeare
Literary Analysis: Dramatic Irony

Dramatic irony is a contradiction between what a character thinks and says and what the audience or reader knows is true. For example, in Act III, Capulet plans Juliet's wedding to Paris. He does not know what you know: that Juliet is already married to Romeo. Dramatic irony involves the audience emotionally in the story.

Shakespeare knew his audience could become *too* involved in the intense emotion of *Romeo and Juliet*. Therefore, he made sure to include the following elements to lighten the play's mood:

- **Comic relief:** a technique used to interrupt a serious scene by introducing a humorous character or situation
- **Puns:** plays on words involving a word with multiple meanings or two words that sound alike but have different meanings. For example, the dying Mercutio makes a pun involving two meanings of the word *grave*: "Ask for me tomorrow, and you shall find me a grave man."

DIRECTIONS: *Use the lines provided to answer the following questions.*

1. Explain the dramatic irony in this passage from Scene i, when Friar Lawrence asks Paris to leave.

    FRIAR. My lord, we must entreat the time alone.
    PARIS. God shield I should disturb devotion!
    Juliet, on Thursday early will I rouse ye.

    _____
    _____

2. In Scene ii, Juliet tells her father she will go through with the wedding, and he begins to make preparations for the celebration. How do Capulet's words create dramatic irony?

    CAPULET. My heart is wondrous light,
    Since this same wayward girl is so reclaimed.

    _____
    _____

3. Juliet prepares for bed in Scene iii. Why is this exchange dramatically ironic?

    LADY CAPULET. What, are you busy, ho? Need you my help?
    JULIET. No, madam; we have culled such necessaries
    As are behoveful for our state tomorrow. . . .
    LADY CAPULET. Good night.
    Get thee to bed, and rest: for thou hast need.

    _____
    _____

Name _____ Date _____

The Tragedy of Romeo and Juliet, Act IV, by William Shakespeare
Reading: Break Down Long Sentences

To understand a long passage of Shakespearean dialogue, you will often find it helpful to **break down long sentences.**

- If a sentence contains multiple subjects or verbs, separate it into smaller sentences with one subject and one verb.
- If a sentence contains colons, semicolons, or dashes, treat those punctuation marks as periods in order to make smaller sentences.

After you have broken down the sentences into smaller units of meaning, put the ideas into a short summary using your own words.

DIRECTIONS: *Mark the following passages with heavy lines to show where you would break down longer sentences. Then, on the lines provided, write a short summary of each passage.*

1. **PARIS.** Immoderately she weeps for Tybalt's death,
   And therefore have I little talked of love;
   For Venus smiles not in a house of tears. (Act IV, Scene i)

   _____
   _____

2. **JULIET.** 'Twixt my extremes and me this bloody knife
   Shall play the umpire, arbitrating that
   Which the commission of thy years and art
   Could to no issue of true honor bring. (Act IV, Scene i)

   _____
   _____

3. **FRIAR.** Hold, daughter. I do spy a kind of hope,
   Which craves as desperate an execution
   As that is desperate which we would prevent.

   _____
   _____
   _____

Name _____ Date _____

The Tragedy of Romeo and Juliet, Act IV, by William Shakespeare
Vocabulary Builder

Word List

dismal   enjoined   loathsome   pensive   vial   wayward

A. Directions: *In each of the following items, think about the meaning of the italicized word and then answer the question.*

1. Would most of the people at a lively party be likely to be in a *pensive* mood? Why or why not?
   _____

2. If a good friend's behavior was *wayward*, would you be pleased or concerned? Explain.
   _____

3. "That place is *dismal*," he remarked. Would you want to go there? Why or why not?
   _____

4. If you were *enjoined* to do something, would the action be ordered or recommended?
   _____

5. If a swampland you were visiting had a *loathsome* smell, would you be tempted to return?
   _____

6. Would a sick person or a well person be more likely to carry a *vial*? Explain.
   _____

B. Word Study: The prefix *en-* means "in" or "cause to be." Answer each of the following questions using one of these words containing *en-*: endanger, enjoined, enlighten, enlarge, entice.

1. What might you be *enjoined* to do in a library?
   _____

2. What might a person *enlarge*?
   _____

3. How might you *entice* your dog to do a trick?
   _____

4. What might *enlighten* you about the subject of medicine?
   _____

5. What might *endanger* swimmers?
   _____

Name _____ Date _____

The Tragedy of Romeo and Juliet, *Act V,* by William Shakespeare
Writing About the Big Question

Do our differences define us?

Big Question Vocabulary

accept	assimilated	background	conformity	culture
defend	determine	differences	differentiate	discriminate
individuality	similarity	understanding	unique	values

A. *Use one or more words from the list above to complete each sentence.*

1. There is often a _____ among superheroes.

2. Many have _____ powers that set them apart from others.

3. They stand up for _____ such as truth, justice, and the American way.

4. They use their powers to _____ good people from evildoers.

B. *Follow the directions in responding to each of the items below.*

1. In two sentences, describe two superpowers you would most like to have to set you apart from others.
   _____
   _____

2. Write two sentences explaining why you would want to have one of the preceding powers. Use at least two of the Big Question vocabulary words.
   _____
   _____

C. *In* The Tragedy of Romeo and Juliet, *two young lovers come from families locked in a deadly feud. That difference defines their relationship and forces the plot toward tragic consequences. Complete the sentence below. Then, write a short paragraph in which you connect this idea to the Big Question.*

One thing that we can learn from the differences we see in others is _____
_____
_____
_____
_____

Name _____ Date _____

The Tragedy of Romeo and Juliet, *Act V*, by William Shakespeare
Literary Analysis: Tragedy and Motive

A **tragedy** is a drama in which the central character, who is of noble stature, meets with disaster or great misfortune. The tragic hero's downfall is usually the result of one of the following:

- fate
- a serious character flaw
- some combination of both

Motive is an important element of a tragic hero's character. A character's motive is the reason behind an individual's thoughts or actions. In many of Shakespeare's tragedies, the hero's motives are basically good, but sometimes misguided. As a result, the hero suffers a tragic fate that may seem undeserved.

Although tragedies typically have unhappy endings, they can also be uplifting. They often show the greatness of which the human spirit is capable when faced with grave challenges.

DIRECTIONS: *Use the lines provided to answer the questions about tragedy and motive in* Romeo and Juliet.

1. In what ways does Romeo or Juliet fit the characteristics of a tragic hero? How does the character *not* fit these characteristics? In your answer, include a consideration of his or her tragic flaw.

   _____
   _____
   _____
   _____
   _____

2. The ancient Greek philosopher Aristotle, in his treatise on tragedy entitled *Poetics*, identified another element that is common to most tragedies: the hero's recognition of the whole tragic situation. This recognition always comes too late for the hero to avoid disaster or death. However, Shakespeare departs from Aristotle's idea about the hero's recognition. In *Romeo and Juliet*, it is not Romeo or Juliet who experiences recognition, but other characters in the play. Who are these characters, and when does the recognition occur?

   _____
   _____
   _____
   _____
   _____
   _____

Name _____ Date _____

The Tragedy of Romeo and Juliet, Act V, by William Shakespeare
Reading: Analyze Causes and Effects

To understand the action in a tragedy, it is often useful to **analyze causes and effects.**

- A *cause* is an event, an action, or a feeling that produces a result.
- An *effect* is the result produced by the cause.

Tragedies often involve a chain of causes and effects that advances the plot and leads to the final tragic outcome. Understanding how one event leads to another will help you to summarize complicated plots like the one in *Romeo and Juliet*.

DIRECTIONS: As you read Act V, fill in the boxes in this chain-of-events graphic organizer. Note that Scene iii has two chains of events. When your chain-of-events graphic is complete, notice how the events in one scene have produced events in later scenes.

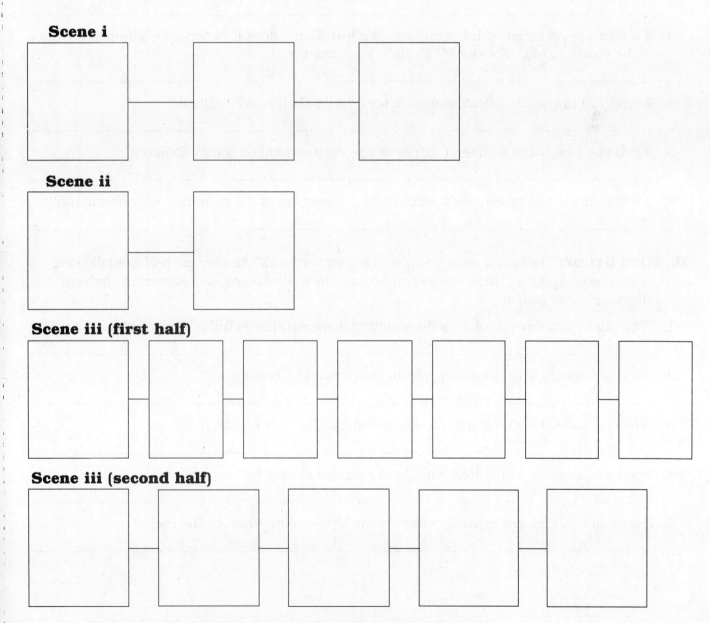

All-in-One Workbook

Name _____ Date _____

The Tragedy of Romeo and Juliet, Act V, by William Shakespeare
Vocabulary Builder

Word List

ambiguities   disperse   haughty   penury   remnants   scourge

A. DIRECTIONS: *In each of the following items, think about the meaning of the italicized word and then answer the question.*

1. Would someone living in *penury* be likely to purchase an expensive new home? Why or why not?
   _____

2. Would the sight of a *scourge* inspire happiness or fear?
   _____

3. If an area is pounded by the *remnants* of a hurricane, does it experience winds in advance of the storm or after the storm? Explain your answer.
   _____

4. Would you praise or criticize someone for *haughty* behavior? Explain.
   _____

5. If you see a crowd at a concert *disperse*, are they coming or going? Explain.
   _____

6. If a statement had *ambiguities*, would you be clear about its meaning? Why or why not?
   _____

B. WORD STUDY: The prefix *ambi-* means "both" or "around." Answer each of the following questions using one of these words containing *ambi-*: *ambience, ambidextrous, ambient, ambiguities, ambivalent*.

1. Why might you have trouble understanding a speech that is full of *ambiguities*?
   _____

2. What are some things that help set the *ambience* of a restaurant?
   _____

3. Why can someone who is *ambidextrous* write with either hand?
   _____

4. What might make you *ambivalent* about taking a course?
   _____

5. If a room has *ambient* lighting, where is the light coming from in the room?
   _____

Name _____ Date _____

The Tragedy of Romeo and Juliet, Act V, by William Shakespeare
Conventions: Parallelism

Parallelism is the use of similar grammatical forms or patterns to express similar ideas. Effective use of parallelism strengthens the connections of your ideas and makes what you say more powerful.

Parallel Construction	Nonparallel	Parallel
Nouns	We donated blankets, clothing, and what people could eat.	We donated blankets, clothing, and food.
Adjectives	The blankets were thick and warm, and they were able to resist fires.	The blankets were thick, warm, and fire resistant.
Verbs	The volunteers gave blood and wrapped bandages, and they had a collection of money.	The volunteers gave blood, wrapped bandages, and collected money.
Prepositional Phrases	People slept on desktops and in chairs, and there were also cots.	People slept on desktops, in chairs, and on cots.
Noun Clauses	Volunteers went to the places needed when they were needed.	Volunteers went where they were needed when they were needed.

A. PRACTICE: *Underline the words that you would change to create parallelism.*

1. We bring food, water, and what we need to repel insects.
2. The places we camp and when we camp are family decisions.
3. We pitch our tent on the ground in a clearing, and there is a brook nearby.

B. WRITING APPLICATION: *On the lines, rewrite these sentences using parallelism.*

1. Daily exercise, a sensible diet, and following a sleep schedule can improve your health.
   _____

2. Try aerobics to improve circulation, to build stamina, and for breathing better.
   _____

3. In yoga, you bend and stretch, with breathing through your nose.
   _____

All-in-One Workbook
© Pearson Education, Inc. All rights reserved.

Name _____ Date _____

The Tragedy of Romeo and Juliet, Act V, by William Shakespeare
Support for Writing to Sources: Argumentative Text

Editorial: For your editorial, use a chart such as the one shown to develop prewriting notes.

Notes on the Prince's Dialogue:
My Opinion of the Prince's Sentencing of Romeo:
Reasons to Support My Opinion:
Details from Act III, Scenes i–iii, to Include in Editorial:
Announcement of Marriage Ceremony:

Persuasive Letter: For your persuasive letter, use a chart such as the one shown to develop prewriting notes.

Opinion Statement (Aim of Letter):
Persuasive Appeals   **1. Factual Evidence:**   **2. Emotional Appeals:**

All-in-One Workbook
© Pearson Education, Inc. All rights reserved.

Name _____ Date _____

The Tragedy of Romeo and Juliet, Act V, by William Shakespeare
Support for Writing to Sources: Persuasive Speech

Use the following chart to list three to five reasons for choosing *The Tragedy of Romeo and Juliet* to be performed by the student body. Next to each reason, write specific support.

Reasons to Choose *Romeo and Juliet*	Evidence to Support the Reason
1 _____	1 _____
2 _____	2 _____
3 _____	3 _____
4 _____	4 _____
5 _____	5 _____

Now, use your notes to write your finished speech, using parallelism and powerful language. When presenting your speech, use proper eye contact and appropriate gestures to emphasize your points.

Name _____ Date _____

The Tragedy of Romeo and Juliet, Act V, by William Shakespeare
Support for Speaking and Listening:
Staged Performance; Mock Trial

Staged Performance: As you prepare your staged performance, take notes on a chart like the one shown.

Scene:
Characters in Scene:
Role Assignments:
Stage Directions:
Critique of My Group's Work:
Critique of Other Groups' Work:

Mock Trial: Together with your group, use the following chart to take notes to prepare for your mock trial.

Role Assignments:
Depositions/Statements:
Questioning/Cross-Examination of Witnesses:

All-in-One Workbook
© Pearson Education, Inc. All rights reserved.

Name _____ Date _____

The Tragedy of Romeo and Juliet, *Act V,* by William Shakespeare
Support for Research and Technology: Presentation of Ideas

16th Century Nobility Research Report: Use this chart to take notes for your annotated flowchart.

Prince Escalus _____	Count Paris _____
_____	_____
_____	_____
_____	_____
Capulets _____	**Montagues** _____
_____	_____
_____	_____
_____	_____

Film Review: Use this chart to develop notes for your film review.

Dance	Music	Camera Angles
_____	_____	_____
_____	_____	_____
_____	_____	_____

Our Opinion of the Film: _____

Reasons to Support Our Opinion: _____

_____

Multimedia Presentation: Use this chart to develop notes for your presentation.

Notes on Act IV, Scene V: _____
_____
Styles / Types of Renaissance Music: _____
_____
Examples of Music to Accompany the Scene: _____
_____
Renaissance Musical Instruments: _____
_____
Sources I Used for Information: _____
_____

Name _____ Date _____

"Pyramus and Thisbe" by Ovid
from A Midsummer Night's Dream by William Shakespeare

Writing About the Big Question

Do our differences define us?

Big Question Vocabulary

accept	assimilated	background	conformity	culture
defend	determine	differences	differentiate	discriminate
individuality	similarity	understanding	unique	values

A. *Use one or more words from the list above to complete each sentence.*

1. Sometimes it is up to the individual to _____ what is right and what is wrong.

2. During World War II, some people would not _____ the Nazi persecution of the Jews.

3. While many did as they were told, a few courageous people refused to act in _____ with oppressive German laws.

4. They showed a true _____ of what it means to be a human being by hiding Jewish people and helping them escape.

B. *Follow the directions in responding to each of the items below.*

1. Write two sentences explaining why it is not always popular to do the right thing.
   _____
   _____

2. Write two sentences explaining how standing up for your beliefs can be considered "courageous." Use at least two of the Big Question vocabulary words.
   _____
   _____

C. *In these selections, the main characters fall victim to love, which is ill-fated due to the differences in characters. Complete the sentence below. Then, write a short paragraph in which you connect this idea to the Big Question.*

When people have major **differences**, love _____
_____
_____
_____
_____

Name _____ Date _____

"Pyramus and Thisbe" by Ovid
The Tragedy of Romeo and Juliet by William Shakespeare
from **A Midsummer Night's Dream** by William Shakespeare

Literary Analysis: Comparing Archetypal Themes—Ill-fated Love

An **archetype** is a plot, a character, an image, or a setting that appears in literature from around the world and throughout history. Archetypes represent truths about life and are said to mirror the working of the human mind. Common archetypes include the following:

- *Characters:* the hero; the outcast
- *Plot types:* the quest, or search; the task
- *Symbol:* water as a symbol for life; fire as a symbol of power

A **theme** is the central idea, message, or insight of a literary work. **Archetypal themes** are those that develop or explore foundational, archetypal ideas. One example of an archetypal theme is ill-fated love, which appears in folklore, mythology, and literature from all over the world.

Works of literature may differ in their presentations of the same archetypal theme for a variety of reasons, including the following:

- the values of the author and the audience at the time the literary work was written
- the author's purpose for writing the literary work
- the culture and language of the author, including any literary styles and expectations

DIRECTIONS: *Write your answers to the following questions on the lines provided.*

1. In what sense are all three of these works stories of ill-fated love: *Romeo and Juliet*, "Pyramus and Thisbe," and the tale of Titania and Bottom's love in *A Midsummer Night's Dream*?

   _____
   _____
   _____

2. Why do you think Shakespeare added Romeo and Juliet's marriage to his story?

   _____
   _____
   _____

3. What message about love does Titania's love for Bottom suggest?

   _____
   _____
   _____

4. Which version of the archetypal theme of ill-fated love do you think best reflects the nature of love? Explain.

   _____
   _____
   _____

Name _____ Date _____

"Pyramus and Thisbe" by Ovid
from A Midsummer Night's Dream by William Shakespeare
Vocabulary Builder

Word List

enamored   enthralled   inevitable   lament

A. DIRECTIONS: *Revise each sentence so that the underlined vocabulary word is used logically. Be sure not to change the vocabulary word.*

1. We heard the mourners' <u>lament</u> and saw them smiling.
   _____

2. Since the defeat of our team in the big game was <u>inevitable</u>, we planned a victory celebration.
   _____

3. Mr. Schuyler nodded his agreement and said he was not <u>enamored</u> of our plan.
   _____

4. We sat <u>enthralled</u> as the lecturer droned on, endlessly repeating himself.
   _____

B. DIRECTIONS: *On the line, write the letter of the choice that is the best antonym, or opposite, for each word.*

___ 1. inevitable
   A. available
   B. presentable
   C. avoidable
   D. grotesque

___ 2. enamored
   A. charmed
   B. gratified
   C. assumed
   D. disgusted

___ 3. enthralled
   A. bored
   B. attracted
   C. devoted
   D. amused

___ 4. lament
   A. predict
   B. celebrate
   C. protest
   D. despise

C. DIRECTIONS: *Choose the pair of words that expresses the same relationship as the pair in capital letters. Write the letter of your choice on the line.*

___ 1. MOURN : LAMENT
   A. delay : accelerate
   B. attempted : failed
   C. convince : discourage
   D. compliment : flatter

___ 2. ENAMORED : LOVER
   A. feline : cow
   B. fuzzy : peach
   C. fantastic : table
   D. dangerous : perilous

Name _____ Date _____

"Pyramus and Thisbe" by Ovid
The Tragedy of Romeo and Juliet by William Shakespeare
from A Midsummer Night's Dream by William Shakespeare
Support for Writing to Sources: Explanatory Essay

Use a chart like the one shown to make prewriting notes for an essay comparing and contrasting Shakespeare's treatment of the characters and events from "Pyramus and Thisbe" in *Romeo and Juliet* and in *A Midsummer Night's Dream*.

	Romeo and Juliet	*A Midsummer Night's Dream*
How Characters from "Pyramus and Thisbe" Affect Archetypal Theme		
How Settings from "Pyramus and Thisbe" Affect Archetypal Theme		
How Shakespeare Wanted Audience to Feel About Ill-fated Love		

Possible Reasons for Exploring the Same Story in a Tragedy and in a Comedy:

_____
_____
_____
_____

Name _____ Date _____

Writing Process
Support for Writing a Comparison-and-Contrast Essay

Prewriting: Gathering Details
Use the following chart to gather and organize details for your essay. Record similarities in the space where the circles overlap, and note differences in the outer sections of the circles.

Drafting: Choosing an Organization
Use the two graphic organizers to select an organization that suits your topic.

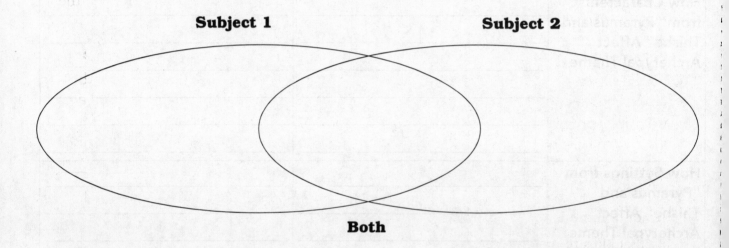

Drafting: Choosing an Organization
Use the two graphic organizers to select an organization that suits your topic.

Point-by-Point Plan

Point 1
- Subject A _____
  _____
- Subject B _____
  _____

Point 2
- Subject A _____
  _____
- Subject B _____
  _____

Subject-by-Subject Plan

Subject A
- Point 1 _____
  _____
- Point 2 _____
  _____

Subject B
- Point 1 _____
  _____
- Point 2 _____
  _____

All-in-One Workbook
© Pearson Education, Inc. All rights reserved.

Writer's Toolbox
Conventions: Combine Sentences with Phrases

To avoid a series of simple sentences, combine some sentences by turning the ideas in one into a phrase in another. An **appositive phrase** clarifies the meaning of a noun or pronoun.

Combine two sentences with an appositive phrase:
   Count Paris wanted to marry Juliet. Paris was a kinsman of Prince Escalus.
   Count Paris, *a kinsman of Prince Escalus*, wanted to marry Juliet.

Verbal phrases use verb forms but act as nouns, adjectives, or adverbs. The chart shows the three types of verbal phrases (*see italics*).

Participial Phrase	Gerund Phrase	Infinitive Phrase
Seeing the sky begin to turn dark, Jared headed for home.	*Playing in the band* takes a lot of her free time.	Andrew's ambition is *to be the best athlete in the game.*
The participial phrase acts as an adjective modifying *Jared*.	The gerund phrase acts as a noun, the subject of the sentence.	The infinitive phrase acts as a predicate nominative after the linking verb *is*.

A. PRACTICE: *Underline the phrase. Then, write the type of phrase* (appositive, participial, gerund, *or* infinitive).

1. Manuel likes to play the piano. _____
2. Playing the piano helps Alice relax. _____
3. Jeremy, a great piano player, will join the band. _____
4. Playing the piano, Ahmed forgets his troubles. _____

B. WRITING APPLICATION: *Combine the two simple sentences in each item into a single sentence by using a verbal phrase or an appositive phrase.*

1. Andrea explores the hills near her home. This activity helps clear her mind.
   _____

2. Joaquin climbed to the top of the hill. He saw the city spread out below.
   _____

3. Denver is a mile above sea level. It is the biggest city in Colorado.
   _____

4. Our students have a goal. They will be the best in the city.
   _____

All-in-One Workbook

Name _____ Date _____

from **The Importance of Being Earnest** by Oscar Wilde
Vocabulary Builder

Selection Vocabulary

    demonstrative   ignorance   indiscretion

A. DIRECTIONS: *Complete each sentence with a word, phrase, or clause that contains a context clue for the italicized word.*

1. I'd like you to be more *demonstrative* with your feelings. For example, I'd like you to _____
_____
_____

2. At the meeting, the man really showed his *ignorance*. He _____
_____
_____
_____

3. He tried to avoid behaving with *indiscretion*. Therefore, he _____
_____
_____
_____

Academic Vocabulary

    ideals   status   ancestry

B. DIRECTIONS: *Write a response to each question. Make sure to use the word in italics at least once in your response.*

1. Is it wrong for a character to judge experiences and friendships based on *ideals*? Explain.
_____
_____

2. In this play, are some characters overly concerned with personal *status*? Explain.
_____
_____

3. His grandparents came from Russia and Australia. How would you describe his *ancestry*?
_____
_____

Name _____ Date _____

from **The Importance of Being Earnest** by Oscar Wilde
Take Notes for Discussion

Before the Group Discussion: Read the following passage from the play. Then, fill out the chart below with ideas you would like to discuss and examples from the text that illustrate your ideas.

> I would strongly advise you, Mr. Worthing, to try and acquire some relations as soon as possible, and to make a definite effort to produce at any rate one parent, of either sex, before the season is quite over.

Discussion Questions	My Ideas	Examples from the Text
1. How would acquiring "some relations" help Jack?		
2. What does Lady Bracknell's line tell you about a key ingredient of social status in Victorian England?		
3. Do you think Oscar Wilde agrees with Lady Bracknell? Explain.		

During the Discussion: As your group discusses each question, take notes on how other students' ideas either differ from or build upon your own.

Discussion Questions	Other Ideas Expressed	Comparison to My Own Ideas
1. How would acquiring "some relations" help Jack?		
2. What does Lady Bracknell's line tell you about a key ingredient of social status in Victorian England?		
3. Do you think Oscar Wilde agrees with Lady Bracknell? Explain.		

All-in-One Workbook
© Pearson Education, Inc. All rights reserved.

Name _____ Date _____

from **The Importance of Being Earnest** by Oscar Wilde
Take Notes for Writing to Sources

Planning Your Informative Text: Before you begin drafting your **character analysis,** use the chart below to organize your ideas. Begin by writing the name of the character you have chosen on the line provided.

Character To Be Analyzed _____

Details and Examples from the Play (from dialogue and stage directions)	How Wilde Used Them to Create a Satire of Victorian Society

All-in-One Workbook
© Pearson Education, Inc. All rights reserved.

Name _____ Date _____

from **The Importance of Being Earnest** by Oscar Wilde
Take Notes for Research

Take Notes: As you research **class structure in Victorian England,** use the forms below to take notes from your sources. As necessary, continue your notes on the back of this page, on note cards, or in a word-processing document.

Source Information Check one: ☐ Primary Source   ☐ Secondary Source

Title: _____ Author: _____

Publication Information: _____

Page(s): _____

Main Idea: _____
_____

Quotation or Paraphrase: _____
_____

Source Information Check one: ☐ Primary Source   ☐ Secondary Source

Title: _____ Author: _____

Publication Information: _____

Page(s): _____

Main Idea: _____
_____

Quotation or Paraphrase: _____
_____

Source Information Check one: ☐ Primary Source   ☐ Secondary Source

Title: _____ Author: _____

Publication Information: _____

Page(s): _____

Main Idea: _____
_____

Quotation or Paraphrase: _____
_____

Name _____ Date _____

"The Necklace," by Guy de Maupassant
Vocabulary Builder

Selection Vocabulary

dejection   disheveled   profoundly

A. DIRECTIONS: *Decide whether each statement below is true or false. On the line before each item, write* **TRUE** *or* **FALSE**. *Then explain your answers.*

_____ 1. If someone felt *dejection*, he or she would probably be smiling broadly.
_____

_____ 2. Someone might appear *disheveled* after wrestling with a large dog.
_____

_____ 3. Someone who is *profoundly* happy might require some help to cheer up.
_____

Academic Vocabulary

estimation   class   elaborate

B. DIRECTIONS: *Write a response to each question. Make sure to use the italicized word at least once in your response.*

1. In your *estimation*, how many books are in the school library?
_____
_____

2. Would multimillionaires be considered members of the middle *class*?
_____
_____

3. Would the summary of a short story *elaborate* on the plot events?
_____
_____

Name _____ Date _____

"The Necklace" by Guy de Maupassant
Take Notes for Discussion

Before the Partner Discussion: Read the following passage from the story.

> Madame Loisel looked old now. She had become the sort of strong woman, hard and coarse, that one finds in poor families. Disheveled, her skirts askew, with reddened hands, she spoke in a loud voice, slopping water over the floors as she washed them. But sometimes, when her husband was at the office, she would sit down by the window and muse over that party long ago when she had been so beautiful, the belle of the ball.

During the Discussion: As you discuss each question, take notes on how your partner's ideas either differ from or build upon your own.

Discussion Questions	Other Ideas Expressed	Comparison to My Own Ideas
2. How does the life Mathilde aspired to compare with the one she creates?		
3. When she muses about the party, do you think her memories are happy?		
3. Does this story teach a lesson? If so, what is that lesson?		

All-in-One Workbook
© Pearson Education, Inc. All rights reserved.

Name _____ Date _____

"The Necklace" by Guy de Maupassant
Take Notes for Research

As you research the **changing social order of France in the nineteenth century,** use the chart below to take notes from your sources. As necessary, continue your notes on the back of this page, on note cards, or in a word-processing document.

Notes for Infographic on Nineteenth-Century France

Main Idea _____
_____
_____
_____

Relevant to Which Social Class _____
_____
_____
_____

Data, Image, or Text _____
_____
_____
_____

Main Idea _____
_____
_____
_____

Relevant to Which Social Class _____
_____
_____
_____

Data, Image, or Text _____
_____
_____
_____

Main Idea _____
_____
_____
_____

Relevant to Which Social Class _____
_____
_____
_____

Data, Image, or Text _____
_____
_____
_____

Main Idea _____
_____
_____
_____

Relevant to Which Social Class _____
_____
_____
_____

Data, Image, or Text _____
_____
_____
_____

All-in-One Workbook
© Pearson Education, Inc. All rights reserved.

Name _____ Date _____

"The Necklace," by Guy de Maupassant
Take Notes for Writing to Sources

Planning Your Explanation: Before you begin drafting your **expository essay,** use the chart below to organize your ideas. Follow the directions at the top of each box.

1. Write a thesis statement based on your analysis of the necklace as a symbol.

2. Write an outline to lay out the points of your analysis.	3. Elaborate on your outline with examples from the story. Use details and direct quotations.

Name _____ Date _____

"New Directions," by Maya Angelou
Vocabulary Builder

Selection Vocabulary

    amicably   balmy   ominous

A. Directions: *Revise each sentence so that the italicized vocabulary word is used logically. Be sure not to change the vocabulary word.*

1. The contestants parted *amicably*, frowning and stamping their feet.
   _____.

2. It was a long walk home, on that *balmy* night, with the icy wind howling at our backs.
   _____.

3. The bright blue sky and the beautiful view were *ominous* signs that this would be a great day.
   _____.

Academic Vocabulary

    emulate   exemplifies   strategy

B. Directions: *Write the letter of the word or phrase that is the best synonym for the italicized word. Then use the italicized word in a complete sentence.*

_____ 1. *strategy*

    A. talent   **B.** assistant   **C.** plan   **D.** vacation

_____ 2. *emulate*

    A. imitate an admired person   **C.** help a needy person

    B. create a new plan   **D.** fail to understand

_____ 3. *exemplifies*

    A. rewards or honors   **C.** is an example of

    B. makes unnecesary   **D.** is superior to

All-in-One Workbook
© Pearson Education, Inc. All rights reserved.

Name _____ Date _____

"New Directions" by Maya Angelou
Take Notes for Discussion

Before the Panel Discussion: Read the following passage from the selection.

> Each of us has the right and the responsibility to assess the roads which lie ahead, and those over which we have traveled, and if the future looms ominous or unpromising, and the roads back uninviting, then we need to gather our resolve and, carrying only the necessary baggage, step off that road into another direction. If the new choice is also unpalatable, without embarrassment, we must be ready to change that as well.

During the Discussion: As you discuss each question, take notes on how other students' ideas either differ from or build upon your own.

Discussion Questions	Other Ideas Expressed	Comparison to My Own Ideas
1. What might be the "necessary baggage" one would carry on a new path?		
2. In what ways is it the individual's right to assess his or her choices in life? In what ways is it a responsibility to chart one's way?		

Name _____ Date _____

"New Directions" by Maya Angelou
Take Notes for Research

As you research the **major events in the Civil Rights or Women's Rights movements,** you can use the organizer below. First, indicate which movement will be your topic. Then use the form to jot down your notes. As necessary, continue your notes on the back of this page, on note cards, or in a word-processing document.

Check one: ☐ Civil Rights movement   ☐ Women's Rights movement

Main Idea _____

Quotation or Paraphrase _____

Source Information _____

Main Idea _____

Quotation or Paraphrase _____

Source Information _____

Main Idea _____

Quotation or Paraphrase _____

Source Information _____

Main Idea _____

Quotation or Paraphrase _____

Source Information _____

Name _____ Date _____

"New Directions," by Maya Angelou
Take Notes for Writing to Sources

Planning Your Argument: Before you begin drafting your **advice column,** use the chart below to organize your ideas. Follow the directions at the top of each box.

---

1. Define *trailblazer* and describe the criteria you used to formulate your definition.

Definition: _____

_____

Criteria: _____

_____

_____

---

2. List the personal qualities that make someone a trailblazer. Use details from the text to summarize what Annie Johnson did and why she is a model for what a trailblazer should be.

_____

_____

_____

_____

_____

_____

_____

_____

_____

_____

---

3. Plan appropriate wording for your advice. Ask yourself: What words and what tone will best encourage my readers to become trailblazers?

_____

_____

_____

_____

_____

_____

_____

_____

_____

_____

Name _____ Date _____

from **Fragile Self-Worth** by Tim Kasser
Vocabulary Builder

Selection Vocabulary

discrepancy   empirical   realm

A. DIRECTIONS: *Decide whether each statement below is true or false. On the line before each item, write TRUE or FALSE. Then explain your answers.*

_____ 1. There is no *discrepancy* between a healthy diet and a fat-filled diet.
_____

_____ 2. *Empirical* data can be based on observations and experiences rather than lengthy experiments or tests.
_____

_____ 3. There is only one *realm* to be concerned with in life, and that is the realm of work.
_____

Academic Vocabulary

compensation   assertions   compelling

B. DIRECTIONS: *Provide an explanation for your answer to each question.*

1. What is a fair hourly rate of *compensation* for working in a fast-food restaurant?
_____
_____

2. Are *assertions* the same as facts?
_____
_____

3. What short story would you consider *compelling*? Explain.
_____
_____

Name _____ Date _____

from **Fragile Self-Worth** by Tim Kasser
Take Notes for Discussion

Before the Group Discussion: Read the following passage from the selection.

> . . . materialistic people over-idealize wealth and possessions and therefore experience discrepancies that cause them to feel dissatisfied and to want further materialistic means of feeling good about themselves. But the satisfactions from this compensation only temporarily improve their sense of worth, and soon they return to another cycle of dissatisfaction.

During the Discussion: As you discuss each question, take notes on how other students' ideas either differ from or build upon your own.

Discussion Questions	Other Ideas Expressed	Comparison to My Own Ideas
1. What does it mean to over-idealize wealth and possessions?		
2. Do your own observations of both real life and television support Kasser's assertions?		
3. What is the difference between striving for a better life and being materialistic?		

All-in-One Workbook
© Pearson Education, Inc. All rights reserved.

Name _____ Date _____

from **Fragile Self-Worth** by Tim Kasser
Take Notes for Research

As you research **the impact of social media on people's materialism and feelings of satisfaction,** you can use the organizer below to take notes from your sources. As necessary, continue your notes on the back of this page, on note cards, or in a word-processing document.

The Impact of Social Media, Including Its Advertising, on People's Materialism and Feelings of Satisfaction

Main Idea _____

Quotation or Paraphrase _____
_____
_____
_____
_____

Source Information _____
_____
_____
_____
_____

Main Idea _____

Quotation or Paraphrase _____
_____
_____
_____
_____

Source Information _____
_____
_____
_____
_____

Main Idea _____

Quotation or Paraphrase _____
_____
_____
_____
_____

Source Information _____
_____
_____
_____
_____

Main Idea _____

Quotation or Paraphrase _____
_____
_____
_____
_____

Source Information _____
_____
_____
_____
_____

Name _____ Date _____

from **Fragile Self-Worth** by Tim Kasser
Take Notes for Writing to Sources

Planning Your Argument: Before you begin drafting your **critical response** to Kasser's argument, use the chart below to organize your ideas.

1. Notes for the Opening Paragraph. (Plan a strong opening statement that summarizes your point of view regarding Kasser's argument. Do you agree or disagree with him? Explain why, using details and knowledge you have gained from your own experiences.)

_____
_____
_____
_____
_____

2. Notes for the Body of Your Critical Response. (List the points that Kasser makes with which you agree or disagree. Include direct quotations from the text. After each one, explain your position.)

_____
_____
_____
_____
_____
_____
_____
_____

3. Notes for the Conclusion. (Restate and deepen your position with strong, direct assertions.)

_____
_____
_____
_____
_____

Name _____ Date _____

"My Possessions Myself" by Russell W. Belk
Vocabulary Builder

Selection Vocabulary

    aggregate   domestic   embellishes

A. DIRECTIONS: *Complete each sentence with a word, phrase, or clause that contains a context clue for the italicized word.*

1. A *domestic* animal is one that _____, and an example is _____.

2. An *aggregate* group of working people might include _____.

3. Items to *embellish* a backpack might include _____.

Academic Vocabulary

    insights   minimize   reasoning

B. DIRECTIONS: *Think about the meaning of each italicized word. Then answer each question with a complete sentence.*

1. In what way do you think characters in literature often provide readers with *insights* into the behavior of people in the real world?
   _____
   _____

2. In "The Necklace," did Mathilde use productive *reasoning* when faced with the central conflict?
   _____
   _____

3. What might people do to *minimize* the amount of trash that overflows our landfills?
   _____
   _____

Name _____ Date _____

"My Possessions Myself" by Russell W. Belk
Take Notes for Discussion

Before the Partner Discussion: Read the following passage from the selection. Then, fill out the chart below with ideas you would like to discuss and examples from the text that support your ideas.

> ...possessions provide a sense of the past. Many studies have shown that the loss of possessions that follows natural disasters or that occurs when elderly people are put in institutions is often traumatic. What people feel in these circumstances is, quite literally, a loss of self.

Discussion Questions	My Ideas	Examples from the Text
1. This passage suggests that a sense of the past is important to a strong sense of identity. Do you agree?		
2. How might cultural differences add to or minimize this strong identification with possessions?		

During the Discussion: As you discuss each question, take notes on how your partner's ideas either differ from or build upon your own.

Discussion Questions	Other Ideas Expressed	Comparison to My Own Ideas
1. This passage suggests that a sense of the past is important to a strong sense of identity. Do you agree?		
2. How might cultural differences add to or minimize this strong identification with possessions?		

All-in-One Workbook

Name _____ Date _____

"My Possessions Myself" by Russell W. Belk

Take Notes for Research

As you research **an ancient culture to discover what "grave goods" reveal about their society,** you can use the organizer below to take notes from your sources. At the top, identify the culture that you have chosen for your topic. Then use the form to collect your information. As necessary, continue your notes on the back of this page, on note cards, or in a word-processing document.

Ancient Culture: _____ .

Main Idea _____

Quotation or Paraphrase _____

Source Information _____

Main Idea _____

Quotation or Paraphrase _____

Source Information _____

Main Idea _____

Quotation or Paraphrase _____

Source Information _____

Main Idea _____

Quotation or Paraphrase _____

Source Information _____

All-in-One Workbook
© Pearson Education, Inc. All rights reserved.

Name _____ Date _____

"My Possessions Myself" by Russell W. Belk
Take Notes for Writing to Sources

Planning Your Argument: Before you begin drafting your **persuasive essay**, use the chart below to organize your ideas.

My Introduction   _____   _____   **Belk's statement:** "Is the fact that we are what we possess desirable or undesirable?"   **My position:** _____   _____   _____   _____   _____
Evidence to Support My Position   **1. from Belk's article:**   _____   _____   _____   _____   _____   **2. from my own observations and experiences:**   _____   _____   _____   _____   _____
My Conclusion (Sum up your strongest point and restate your position.)   _____   _____   _____   _____

Name _____ Date _____

Cartoon from *The New Yorker*
Vocabulary Builder and Writing to Sources

Academic Vocabulary

    depicted   incongruity

DIRECTIONS: *Complete each sentence with a word, phrase, or clause that contains a context clue for the underlined word.*

1. Let me describe the <u>incongruity</u> between Harold's behavior and his words. He _____.

2. I felt that the people <u>depicted</u> in that painting were strange because _____.

Take Notes for Writing to Sources

Planning Your Narrative: Before you begin drafting your **short story,** use the chart below to organize your ideas. Follow the directions at the top of each box.

1. Jot down details you will use to describe the man's life before this scene takes place.
2. Draft the conversation that leads up to this scene.
3. Jot down details regarding a conflict or problem that takes place. Use dialogue and vivid details.
4. Draft a conclusion to the story. Tell how the conflict is resolved.

All-in-One Workbook
© Pearson Education, Inc. All rights reserved.

Unit 5: Themes in Literature
Big Question Vocabulary—1

The Big Question: Do heroes have responsibilities?

Small children who watch a superhero on television will often pattern their behavior after the superhero's behavior.

honesty: truthfulness, sincerity

justice: fairness

morality: conformity to the rules of proper conduct

responsibility: reliability or dependability

wisdom: good sense and judgment, especially based on life experience

DIRECTIONS: *Create a superhero that little children could respect and admire. For each of the vocabulary words, give an example of how your superhero would demonstrate this quality. Use each vocabulary word in each description.*

HONESTY: _____
_____
_____

JUSTICE: _____
_____
_____

MORALITY: _____
_____
_____

RESPONSIBILITY: _____
_____
_____

WISDOM: _____
_____
_____

Name _____ Date _____

Unit 5: Themes in Literature
Big Question Vocabulary—2

The Big Question: Do heroes have responsibilities?

Often an athlete, a movie star, or a politician will be regarded as a hero. With that hero status comes a responsibility to act in a way that is consistent with good values.

character: a combination of valued qualities, such as honesty and integrity

hero: a person of great courage who is admired for his actions

imitate: to copy the way someone else behaves and/or speaks

intentions: purposes or plans of someone's actions or behavior

serve: to be useful or helpful

DIRECTIONS: *Think of a public figure whom you consider a hero. Answer the following questions using the vocabulary words that are in parentheses.*

1. Who is the public figure you selected? (*hero*)
   _____

2. What qualities does this person have that make him or her admirable? (*character*)
   _____
   _____

3. How is this person useful or helpful to the world or to a particular community? (*serve*)
   _____
   _____

4. What do you suppose this person's aims are with regard to the world or his or her community? (*intentions*)
   _____
   _____

5. In what ways have you and others learned from this person? (*imitate*)
   _____
   _____

Name _____ Date _____

Unit 5: Themes in Literature
Big Question Vocabulary—3

 The Big Question: Do heroes have responsibilities?

If we look around our communities, we will often discover that there are "unsung heroes," or people who do not get recognition for their exceptional actions.

choices: decisions

identify: to recognize and name something

involvement: taking part in an activity or event

obligation: moral or legal duty

standard: level of quality, skill, or ability that is acceptable in a particular situation

DIRECTIONS: *Recognize someone in your community who is an "unsung hero" by creating a plaque to award him or her. In the plaque, describe your hero's achievements using all the vocabulary words. Your hero can be real or imagined.*

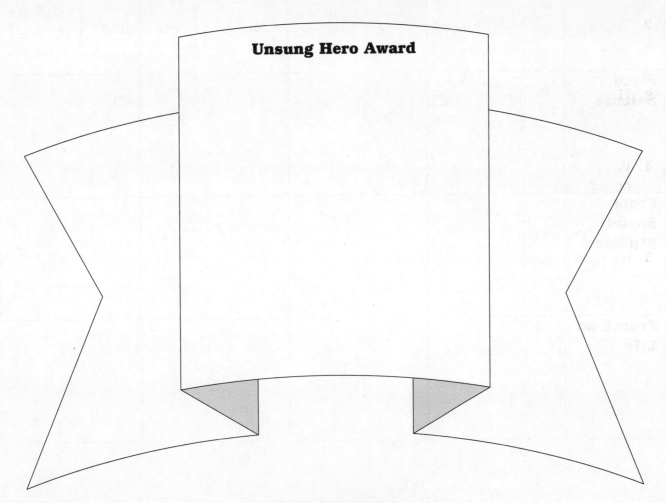

Name _____ Date _____

Unit 5: Themes in Literature
Applying the Big Question

The Big Question: Do heroes have responsibilities?

DIRECTIONS: Complete the chart below to apply what you have learned about heroes and their responsibilities. One row has been completed for you.

Example	The heroic act	Motivation for the act	The hero's responsibilities	What I learned
From Literature	In "Odysseus' Revenge" in the *Odyssey*, Odysseus kills his wife's suitors.	His sense of outrage and vengeance	To protect his wife, son, and the people of Ithaca	Heroes may have divided responsibilities and may give in to their emotions.
From Literature				
From Science				
From Social Studies				
From Real Life				

All-in-One Workbook
© Pearson Education, Inc. All rights reserved.

Name _____ Date _____

from the Odyssey, Part 1 by Homer
Writing About the Big Question

 Do heroes have responsibilities?

Big Question Vocabulary

character	choices	hero	honesty	identify
imitate	intentions	involvement	justice	morality
obligation	responsibility	serve	standard	wisdom

A. *Use one or more words from the list above to complete each sentence.*

1. The _____ made by a(n) _____ in a literary work often determine the outcome of the plot.

2. A(n) _____ is usually someone who embodies the values of an entire culture or society.

3. _____ and _____ are two values that a(n) _____ typically upholds.

4. By any measure, Odysseus in Homer's *Odyssey* lives up to a heroic _____.

5. It is usually easy to _____ the hero of an epic poem.

B. *Follow the directions in responding to each of the items below.*

1. List two different times when you became aware of a **responsibility.**
   _____
   _____

2. Write two sentences to explain one of these experiences, and describe how it made you feel. Use at least two of the Big Question vocabulary words.
   _____
   _____

C. *Complete the sentences below. Then, write a short paragraph in which you connect the sentences to the Big Question.*

A **hero** has an **obligation** to _____. The **choices** he or she makes must _____.

_____
_____
_____
_____

Name _____ Date _____

from the Odyssey, Part 1 by Homer
Literary Analysis: Epic Hero

An **epic hero** is the larger-than-life central character in an epic—a long narrative poem about important events in the history or folklore of a nation or culture. Through adventurous deeds, the epic hero demonstrates traits—such as loyalty, honor, and resourcefulness—that are valued by the society in which the epic originates.

Many epics begin *in medias res* ("in the middle of things"), meaning that much of the important action in the story occurred before the point at which the poem begins. Therefore, an epic hero's adventures are often recounted in a **flashback,** a scene that interrupts the sequence of events in a narrative to relate earlier events. Flashbacks also allow the poet to provide a more complete portrait of the epic hero's character.

DIRECTIONS: Consider the adventures shown in the left column of the following chart. Then, determine what evidence is contained in each adventure to support the position that Odysseus has the superior physical and mental prowess to be an epic hero. Write your answers in the chart.

Adventure	Evidence of Mental Prowess	Evidence of Physical Prowess
1. The Lotus-Eaters		
2. The Cyclops		
3. The Sirens		
4. Scylla and Charybdis		

All-in-One Workbook
© Pearson Education, Inc. All rights reserved.

Name _____ Date _____

from the Odyssey, *Part 1* by Homer
Reading: Analyze the Influence of Historical and Cultural Context

The **historical and cultural context** of a work is the backdrop of details of the time and place in which the work is set or in which it was written. These details include the events, beliefs, and customs of a specific culture and time. When you read a work from another time and culture, **use background and prior knowledge** to analyze the influence of the historical and cultural context.

- Read the author biography, footnotes, and other textual aids to understand the work's historical and cultural context.
- Note how characters' behavior and attitudes reflect that context.

DIRECTIONS: *Answer the following questions on the lines provided.*

1. What does the common noun *odyssey* mean? Use a dictionary, if necessary, to look up this word and identify its meaning. How does this word relate to Homer's epic and the hero Odysseus?

    _____
    _____
    _____

2. What does the word *Homeric* mean? How does this word relate to the ancient Greek epics the *Iliad* and the *Odyssey*?

    _____
    _____
    _____

3. About when were the Homeric epics composed, or when did they assume their final form after centuries of development in the oral tradition?

    _____

4. Reread Odysseus' description of the Cyclopes in Part 1, lines 109–120. What does this passage imply about ancient Greek values and beliefs? Explain your answer in a brief paragraph.

    _____
    _____
    _____
    _____
    _____
    _____
    _____

Name _____ Date _____

from the Odyssey, Part 1 by Homer
Vocabulary Builder

Word List

ardor   assuage   bereft   dispatched   insidious   plundered

A. DIRECTIONS: *In each of the following items, think about the meaning of the italicized word and then answer the question.*

1. If you regard someone as *insidious*, do you like or dislike that person? Why?
   _____

2. Historically, when do people tend to *plunder*—during wartime or peacetime?
   _____

3. If Maria *dispatched* her assignment, did it take her a long time or a short time to finish?
   _____

4. Would you use gentle words or provocative words to *assuage* someone's anger or demands? Explain.
   _____

5. If you lose your *ardor*, do you feel eager or unenthusiastic?
   _____

6. If a cough leaves someone *bereft* of breath, is the person breathing normally or poorly?
   _____

B. WORD STUDY: *The Old English prefix* be-, *meaning "around," "make," or "covered with," can sometimes be added to a noun or an adjective to create a transitive verb. Examples include* beheld *and* begone. *Match the word in Column A with its meaning in Column B by writing the correct letter on the line provided.*

___ 1. bemoan   A. be on one's guard
___ 2. bewilder   B. lament
___ 3. beware   C. signify
___ 4. betoken   D. confuse
___ 5. bereft   E. deprived

Name _____   Date _____

from the Odyssey, *Part 1* by Homer
Conventions: Simple and Compound Sentences

A **simple sentence** consists of a single independent clause. Although a simple sentence is just one independent clause with one subject and verb, the subject, verb, or both may be compound. A simple sentence may have modifying phrases and complements. However, it cannot have a dependent clause.

> **Example:** Odysseus returned to Ithaca and took his revenge on the suitors. (simple sentence with compound verb)

A **compound sentence** consists of two or more independent clauses. The clauses can be joined by a comma and a coordinating conjunction or by a semicolon. Like a simple sentence, a compound sentence contains no dependent clauses.

> **Example:** The suitors reveled in the hall; in the meantime, Penelope questioned the disguised Odysseus.

A. DIRECTIONS: *Identify each sentence as simple or compound.*

1. In his monumental epic, the *Odyssey*, Homer recounts the wanderings of Odysseus on his journey home to Ithaca after the Trojan War. _____
2. Odysseus enjoys the favor of the goddess Athena, but his safe return is jeopardized by the hostility of Poseidon, the sea god. _____
3. Odysseus foolishly leads his men into the cave of the Cyclops; there, several of them meet a ghastly fate. _____
4. Odysseus tricks the Cyclops by telling him a false name: "Nohbdy." _____
5. At the end of this adventure, however, Odysseus boastfully reveals his true name, thereby making himself vulnerable to the Cyclops' curse. _____

B. WRITING APPLICATION: *On the following lines, write a paragraph in which you describe what you would wish for if you had three wishes. In your writing, use both simple and compound sentences. Be prepared to identify each type of sentence.*

_____
_____
_____
_____
_____
_____
_____
_____
_____
_____

Name _____ Date _____

from the Odyssey, Part 1 by Homer
Support for Writing to Sources: Narrative Text (Retelling)

Use a chart like the one below to jot down notes for your everyday epic.

Everyday Event: _____
_____

Epic Dimensions (adventure, bravery, life-and-death challenges): _____
_____
_____
_____
_____

Multiple Points of View: _____
_____
_____
_____

Supernatural/Fantastic Elements: _____
_____
_____
_____
_____

Ideas for Performance/Recitation: _____
_____
_____
_____
_____

Name _____ Date _____

from the Odyssey, Part 1 by Homer
Support for Speaking and Listening: Conversation

Use the following lines to make notes for your everyday conversation.

Odysseus' Exploits

The Lotus-Eaters: _____
_____

The Cyclops: _____
_____

The Land of the Dead: _____
_____

The Sirens: _____
_____

Scylla and Charybdis: _____
_____

The Cattle of the Sun God: _____
_____

Ancient Greek Values Shown in the *Odyssey*

Courage: _____
_____

Intelligence: _____
_____

Respect for the Gods: _____
_____

Leadership: _____
_____

Name _____ Date _____

from the Odyssey, Part 2 by Homer
Writing About the Big Question

 Do heroes have responsibilities?

Big Question Vocabulary

character	choices	hero	honesty	identify
imitate	intentions	involvement	justice	morality
obligation	responsibility	serve	standard	wisdom

A. *Use one or more words from the list above to complete each sentence.*

1. One definition of a(n) _____ is that he or she is someone whom large numbers of people would like to _____.

2. Many epics focus on a hero's _____ in a journey or quest.

3. Our _____ were good, but we could not steer the project to a successful outcome.

4. In epic narratives, heroes often profit from the _____ of a god, sage, or prophet.

5. Responsible politicians usually feel a(n) _____ to the voters who elected them.

B. *Follow the directions in responding to each of the items below.*

1. List two different times when you had to decide between two very different **choices**.
   _____
   _____

2. Write two sentences to explain one of these experiences, and describe how it made you feel. Use at least two of the Big Question vocabulary words.
   _____
   _____

C. *Complete the sentence below. Then, write a short paragraph in which you connect the sentences to the Big Question.*

The true **character** of a **hero** can be seen in _____
_____
_____
_____
_____

Name _____ Date _____

from the Odyssey, Part 2 by Homer
Literary Analysis: Epic Simile

An **epic simile** is an elaborate comparison that may extend for several lines. Epic similes may use the words *like, as, just as,* or *so* to make the comparison. Unlike a normal simile, which draws a comparison to a single distinct image, an epic simile is longer and more involved. It might recall an entire place or story. Epic similes are sometimes called Homeric similes.

DIRECTIONS: *Read the epic similes that follow. Then, circle the letter of the answer that best completes each sentence.*

A. But the man skilled in all ways of contending,
satisfied by the great bow's look and heft,
like a musician, like a harper, when
with quiet hand upon his instrument
he draws between his thumb and forefinger
a sweet new string upon a peg: so effortlessly
Odysseus in one motion strung the bow.

1. Complete this analogy to show the extended comparison Homer makes in this epic simile:
   archer : bow ::
   A. composer : instrument.
   B. peg : string.
   C. musician : harp.
   D. hand : forefinger.

2. The comparison suggests that Odysseus
   A. is nervous before he begins.
   B. is as adept and graceful as a musician.
   C. is proficient in music.
   D. is always satisfied.

B. Think of a catch that fishermen haul in to a half-moon bay
in a fine-meshed net from the whitecaps of the sea:
how all are poured out on the sand, in throes for the salt sea,
twitching their cold lives away in Helios' fiery air:
so lay the suitors heaped on one another.

1. Complete this analogy to show the extended comparison Homer makes in this epic simile:
   Odysseus : suitors ::
   A. big fish : little fish.
   B. hunter : catch.
   C. Odysseus : enemies.
   D. fishermen : fish.

2. The comparison suggests that
   A. Odysseus is also a good fisherman.
   B. the suitors have as much chance against Odysseus as fish have when they are caught in a net.
   C. something fishy is going on in Ithaca, and Odysseus must correct it.
   D. the setting of much of the epic is the Greek isles, where fishing is an important industry.

Name _____ Date _____

from the Odyssey, *Part 2* by Homer
Reading: Analyze the Influence of Historical and Cultural Context

The **historical and cultural context** of a work is the backdrop of details of the time and place in which the work is set or in which it was written. These details include the events, beliefs, and customs of a specific culture and time. When you **identify influences on your own reading and responses,** the historical and cultural context reflected in a work becomes more apparent.

- As you read a work from another time and culture, keep your own beliefs and customs in mind.
- Notice the ways in which your reactions to ideas and situations in the work differ from the reactions of the characters.
- Consider whether your reactions reflect your own cultural values.

DIRECTIONS: *For each of the following events or elements in Part 2 of the* Odyssey, *write a few notes on the historical and cultural context. Pay special attention to whether the event or element seems to reflect a universal value or belief or whether it seems specifically rooted in the cultural context of ancient Greece.*

1. Odysseus' reunion with Telemachus
   _____
   _____
   _____

2. the episode focusing on Odysseus' dog, Argus
   _____
   _____
   _____

3. the laziness and arrogance of the suitors
   _____
   _____
   _____

4. Odysseus' and Penelope's testing of each other
   _____
   _____
   _____

5. Odysseus' slaughter of the suitors
   _____
   _____
   _____

All-in-One Workbook
© Pearson Education, Inc. All rights reserved.

Name _____ Date _____

from the Odyssey, Part 2 by Homer
Vocabulary Builder

Word List

   bemusing   contempt   dissemble   equity   incredulity   maudlin

A. DIRECTIONS: *In each of the following items, think about the meaning of the italicized word and then answer the question.*

1. From whom would you reasonably expect *equity*—a judge or a thief?
   _____

2. Would you treat someone whom you admire with *contempt*? Why or why not?
   _____

3. Does being *maudlin* involve your intelligence or your emotions? Explain your answer.
   _____

4. What kind of story or report would inspire *incredulity* in you? Explain.
   _____

5. Would you react to a long, *bemusing* lecture with enthusiasm or with annoyance?
   _____

6. Would someone trying to *dissemble* be forthright or insincere?
   _____

B. DIRECTIONS: *Use the context of the sentences and what you know about the Latin prefix dis- to explain your answer to each question.*

1. If one high school football team *displaces* another in the league rankings, what happens?
   _____

2. If you *disentangle* a complex problem, what have you done: solved it, or made it worse?
   _____

3. If two plays or novels are *dissimilar*, are they more notable for their likenesses or their differences?
   _____

Name _____ Date _____

from the Odyssey, *Part 2* by Homer
Conventions: Complex and Compound-Complex Sentences

A **complex sentence** consists of one independent clause, which can stand by itself as a sentence, and at least one dependent clause, which cannot stand by itself as a sentence. A **compound-complex sentence** consists of two or more independent clauses and one or more dependent clauses.

Complex sentence: After Odysseus gave Telemachus the signal, Telemachus removed the weapons from the hall.

Compound-complex sentence: Scholars, who live throughout the world, disagree about whether the epics were composed by the same person, and they also wonder about Homer's historical existence.

A. Directions: *Identify each sentence as complex or compound-complex.*

1. Although Odysseus is in disguise, his old dog Argus recognizes him instinctively.
   _____

2. The suitors, who have competed to marry Penelope, behave arrogantly, and they conspire to murder Odysseus' son and heir, Telemachus.
   _____

3. Odysseus becomes anxious when Penelope questions him about the marriage bed.
   _____

4. The *Odyssey*, which has entertained audiences for thousands of years, contains many universal themes; its broad appeal can be explained by Homer's profound understanding of human nature.
   _____

B. Writing Application: *On the following lines, write a paragraph in which you describe a gift that you would like to present to a loved one. In your writing, use all four types of sentences that have been mentioned: simple, compound, complex, and compound-complex. Be prepared to identify each type of sentence.*

_____
_____
_____
_____
_____
_____
_____
_____

Name _____ Date _____

from the Odyssey, *Part 2* by Homer
Support for Writing to Sources: Informative Text (Biography)

Use a chart like the one shown to make notes for your biography of Odysseus.

Events That Reveal Odysseus' Character

1. _____
_____
_____

2. _____
_____
_____

3. _____
_____
_____

4. _____
_____
_____

5. _____
_____
_____

Quotations From the Epic

1. _____
_____
_____

2. _____
_____
_____

3. _____
_____
_____

Name _____ Date _____

from the **Odyssey,** *Part 2* by Homer
Support for Speaking and Listening: Debate

Use a chart such as the one shown to make notes for your debate on the prosecution of Odysseus for killing Penelope's suitors.

Debate Teams: _____

Arguments for the Prosecution

1. _____

2. _____

3. _____

Arguments for the Defense

1. _____

2. _____

3. _____

Name _____ Date _____

Poetry by Edna St. Vincent Millay, Margaret Atwood,
Derek Walcott, and Constantine Cavafy

Writing About the Big Question

Do heroes have responsibilities?

Big Question Vocabulary

character	choices	hero	honesty	identify
imitate	intentions	involvement	justice	morality
obligation	responsibility	serve	standard	wisdom

A. *Use one or more words from the list above to complete each sentence.*

1. A person's individual _____, or code of ethics, is often apparent in the _____ that he or she makes at moments of decision.

2. During the civil rights movement of the 1950s and 1960s, Dr. Martin Luther King, Jr., was one of our nation's most stirring spokesmen for social _____.

3. Since heroes usually embody values we all admire, most of us would like to _____ them.

4. In the legends of King Arthur, Merlin was an elderly sage whose good advice made him famous for his _____.

B. *Follow the directions in responding to each of the items below.*

1. List two occasions on which you felt that you, or someone you know, failed to receive **justice.**
   _____
   _____

2. Write two sentences to explain one of these experiences. Use at least two of the Big Question vocabulary words.
   _____
   _____

C. *Complete the sentences below. Then, write a short paragraph in which you connect the experience to the Big Question.*

In my own life, I know I am responsible for _____. If I do not live up to this **obligation,** one consequence might be _____. When I make responsible **choices,** one positive result is _____.

_____
_____
_____

All-in-One Workbook
© Pearson Education, Inc. All rights reserved.

Name _____ Date _____

Poetry by Edna St. Vincent Millay, Margaret Atwood, Derek Walcott, and Constantine Cavafy
Literary Analysis: Contemporary Interpretations

The characters and events of Homer's *Odyssey* are timeless and universal in their appeal and meaning and have inspired many contemporary interpretations. A **contemporary interpretation** of a literary work is a new piece of writing, such as a poem, story, or play, that a modern-day author bases on an ancient work. An **allusion** is a reference to a well-known person, place, event, literary work, or work of art. By reinventing Homer's tales or by making allusions to them, modern-day writers shed new light on Homer's ancient words. Contemporary interpretations may allude to any aspects of Homer's epic, including plot, characters, settings, imagery and language, and theme.

Even when they are based on the same work, contemporary interpretations can differ widely in purpose and theme. The cultural and historical backgrounds, ideas, attitudes, and beliefs of the contemporary writers profoundly affect their perceptions of the ancient work and the new writings that result.

DIRECTIONS: *Circle the letter of the answer that best completes the sentence.*

1. In Edna St. Vincent Millay's "An Ancient Gesture," the speaker focuses most closely on
   A. Odysseus' travels and the hero's relationships to the gods.
   B. the anguish of Odysseus' son Telemachus.
   C. Penelope's inner grief and frustration at Odysseus' long absence.
   D. the devastation wrought by the Trojan War.

2. In "Siren Song," Margaret Atwood's interpretation of the Sirens suggests that
   A. women are much more complex than they have been given credit for.
   B. the poet herself is not very clever.
   C. men are more clever than they think they are.
   D. women enjoy the roles they play.

3. In "Prologue" and "Epilogue" to the *Odyssey,* Derek Walcott suggests that Billy Blue
   A. has confused the chronological sequence of Odysseus' adventures.
   B. is a modern-day version of Homer, singing the adventures of a "main-man" hero.
   C. believes that we are all capable of behaving as heroically as Odysseus did.
   D. has misinterpreted the character of Penelope.

4. In "Ithaca," Constantine Cavafy sees the wanderings of Odysseus as representing
   A. a grand vacation to exotic places.
   B. the journey through life itself.
   C. a voyage of discovery made possible by such modern conveniences as a credit card.
   D. a trip without a real purpose.

5. In "Ithaca," the lines "Always keep Ithaca fixed in your mind, / . . . But do not hurry the voyage at all" suggest that
   A. the journey is more important than the destination.
   B. we need to know where we are going in life.
   C. everyone should have a home.
   D. some places always remain the same, no matter how other places may change.

Name _____ Date _____

Poetry by Edna St. Vincent Millay, Margaret Atwood, Derek Walcott, and Constantine Cavafy

Vocabulary Builder

Word List

authentic   defrauded   lofty   picturesque   siege

A. DIRECTIONS: *Revise each sentence so that the underlined vocabulary word is used logically. Be sure not to change the vocabulary word.*

1. They refused to buy the old silver coin because they believe it is authentic.
   _____

2. Because the landscape was so picturesque, we did not bother to take any photographs.
   _____

3. The siege of the city was successful, so the soldiers outside the walls retreated.
   _____

4. Because he is a person of lofty ideals, we criticize him harshly.
   _____

5. As a merchant with great integrity, he always defrauded his customers.
   _____

B. DIRECTIONS: *On the line, write the letter of the choice that is the best synonym for each numbered word.*

___ 1. defrauded
    A. rejected
    B. praised
    C. cheated
    D. promoted

___ 2. lofty
    A. illusory
    B. pretentious
    C. drafty
    D. noble

___ 3. authentic
    A. genuine
    B. antique
    C. practical
    D. sentimental

___ 4. siege
    A. strong grip
    B. armed blockade
    C. military alliance
    D. crisis intervention

___ 5. picturesque
    A. grotesque
    B. paradoxical
    C. prevalent
    D. charming

Name _____ Date _____

Poetry by Edna St. Vincent Millay, Margaret Atwood, Derek Walcott, and Constantine Cavafy
Support for Writing to Sources: Explanatory Text

For each poem in this section, use a chart like the one shown to make prewriting notes for an essay focusing on ways in which each poet draws upon the *Odyssey* to communicate a message suited to today's world.

Title of Work: _____
_____
Classical allusion(s) used: _____
Contemporary conflict/situation addressed: _____
Additions by contemporary writer: _____
My personal response: _____

Name _____ Date _____

Writing Process
Support for Writing an Autobiographical Narrative

Prewriting: Gathering Details

Use the chart below to gather and organize details for your autobiographical narrative.

Sequence of Events	Problem or Conflict	Details of Specific Places or Scenes	My Thoughts or Feelings About the Incident

Name _____ Date _____

Writer's Toolbox
Conventions: Sentences with Adverb Clauses

You can sometimes combine related sentences by turning one into a dependent clause. A **clause** is a group of words with a subject and a verb. An **independent clause** expresses a complete thought and can stand alone as a sentence. A **dependent clause** does not express a complete thought and must be linked to an independent clause to form a full sentence. An **adverb clause** is a dependent clause that begins with a subordinating conjunction and modifies a verb, an adjective, or another adverb. Here are some common subordinating conjunctions.

Relationship	Subordinating Conjunctions	Conjunctions Example
time	after, as, as soon as, before, since, until, when, whenever	Travel by boat becomes impossible *after the waterways freeze.*
space/position	where, wherever	Dogsleds travel *where cars cannot go*
cause and effect	as, because, in order that, so that, since	*Because the days end early,* people need artificial light.
condition	if, unless, whether, whether or not	*If the streets are very icy,* some people use cross-country skis.
contrast	although, even though, though, while	*Although winter is a dark time in Alaska,* summers have light almost all night.
comparison	as if, as though	People in winter walk carefully, *as if they are about to topple over.*

A. DIRECTIONS: *Underline the subordinating conjunction that combines the two sentences.*

1. Wear layers of warm clothing (if, although) the weather is cold.
2. Layers provide the best insulation (because, as if) heat is trapped between them.
3. Extremities like hands and ears can get frostbite (where, until) they are exposed.
4. It is important to keep your head and ears covered (when, so that) temperatures drop.

B. WRITING APPLICATION: *For each item, combine the two simple sentences into a single sentence using an adverb clause.*

1. You travel to a much higher altitude. Your body may take time to adjust. (time)

   _____

2. Your breath may be shorter. The air is thinner. (cause and effect)

   _____

3. Denver is a mile above sea level. Pike's Peak is much higher. (contrast)

   _____

Name _____ Date _____

from **The Ramayana**, retold by R. K. Narayan
Vocabulary Builder

Selection Vocabulary
benediction   intolerable   obstinate

A. DIRECTIONS: *Complete each sentence with a word, phrase, or clause that contains a context clue for the italicized word.*

1. To help people facing the *intolerable* conditions, the agency _____
_____

2. The Roman soldiers asked for the *benediction* because _____
_____

3. *Obstinate* group members are difficult to handle because _____
_____

Academic Vocabulary
chaos   embodiment   rationality

B. DIRECTIONS: *Write a response to each question. Make sure to use the word in italics at least once in your response.*

1. When faced with *chaos*, what is an effective way to react? _____
_____

2. Why is *rationality* an important trait in a leader? _____
_____

3. He described his captain as the *embodiment* of courage. What did he mean?
_____
_____

Name _____ Date _____

from **The Ramayana**, retold by R. K. Narayan
Take Notes for Discussion

Before the Group Discussion: Read the following passage from the selection.

Every moment, news came to Ravana of fresh disasters in his camp. One by one, most of his commanders were lost. No one who went forth with battle cries was heard of again. Cries and shouts and the wailings of the widows of warriors came over the chants and songs of triumph that his courtiers arranged to keep up at a loud pitch in his assembly hall. Ravana became restless and abruptly left the hall and went up on a tower, from which he could obtain a full view of the city. He surveyed the scene below but could not stand it. One who had spent a lifetime in destruction, now found the gory spectacle intolerable. Groans and wailings reached his ears with deadly clarity. . . . This was too much for him. He felt a terrific rage rising within him, mixed with some admiration for Rama's valor. He told himself, "The time has come for me to act by myself again."

During the Discussion: As your group discusses each question, take notes on how other students' ideas either differ from or build upon your own.

Discussion Questions	Other Responses	Comparison to My Responses
1. Why might Ravana admire Rama?		
2. Does Ravana seem wholly evil in this passage? Why or why not?		
3. What might Ravana, in his rage, represent?		

Name _____ Date _____

from **The Ramayana**, retold by R. K. Narayan
Take Notes for Writing to Sources

Planning Your Comparison and Contrast: Before you begin drafting your **comparison-and-contrast essay,** use the chart below to organize your ideas. The first column lists characteristics. Use the second column to jot down characteristics of Rama, and use the third column to jot down characteristics of Ravana. Then use your notes to draft an essay in which you explore what each character means in the epic's presentation of **good versus evil.**

Characteristics	Characteristics of Rama	Characteristics of Ravana
1. Thoughts		
2. Feelings		
3. Actions		
4. Words		

Name _____ Date _____

from **The Ramayana,** retold by R. K. Narayan
Take Notes for Research

As you research **Rama's story,** use the forms below to take notes from your sources. As necessary, continue your notes on the back of this page, on note cards, or in a word-processing document.

Source Information Check one: ☐ Primary Source ☐ Secondary Source

Title: _____ Author: _____

Publication Information: _____

Page(s): _____

Main Idea: _____

_____

Quotation or Paraphrase: _____

_____

Source Information Check one: ☐ Primary Source ☐ Secondary Source

Title: _____ Author: _____

Publication Information: _____

Page(s): _____

Main Idea: _____

_____

Quotation or Paraphrase: _____

_____

Source Information Check one: ☐ Primary Source ☐ Secondary Source

Title: _____ Author: _____

Publication Information: _____

Page(s): _____

Main Idea: _____

_____

Quotation or Paraphrase: _____

_____

Name _____ Date _____

"Perseus" by Edith Hamilton
Vocabulary Builder

Selection Vocabulary

    kindred   mortified   revelry

A. DIRECTIONS: *Decide whether each statement below is true or false. On the line before each item, write TRUE or FALSE. Then explain your answers.*

_____ 1. It would be unusual for *kindred* to resemble each other.

_____

_____ 2. A renowned baseball player would probably feel *mortified* if he made a terrible error during an important game.

_____

_____ 3. On the Fourth of July, it is important to avoid any *revelry*.

_____

Academic Vocabulary

    rife   universal

B. DIRECTIONS: *Write a response to each question. Make sure to use the italicized word at least once in your response.*

1. Would a *universal* truth be accepted by many people or only a few people? Explain.

_____

_____

2. With what kind of conflicts is mythology *rife*?

_____

_____

Name _____ Date _____

"Perseus" by Edith Hamilton
Take Notes for Discussion

Before the Group Discussion: Read the following passage from the selection. Then, fill out the chart below with ideas you would like to discuss and examples from the text that support your ideas.

> He had nothing he could give. He was young and proud and keenly mortified. He stood up before them all and did exactly what the King had hoped he would do, declared that he would give him a present better than any there. He would go off and kill Medusa and bring back her head as his gift.

Discussion Questions	My Ideas	Examples from the Text
1. In what ways does Perseus combine the qualities of an ordinary person with those of a hero?		
2. Assess Perseus' plan for killing Medusa. Is it sensible? Why or why not?		

During the Discussion: As you discuss each question, take notes on how your group members' ideas either differ from or build upon your own.

Discussion Questions	Other Ideas Expressed	Comparison to My Own Ideas
1. In what ways does Perseus combine the qualities of an ordinary person with those of a hero?		
2. Assess Perseus' plan for killing Medusa. Is it sensible? Why or why not?		

All-in-One Workbook

Name _____ Date _____

"Perseus" by Edith Hamilton
Take Notes for Research

As you research a **hero or heroine from Greek mythology,** use the chart below to take notes from your sources. Begin by writing the name of the hero or heroine you have chosen on the line at the top of the chart. As necessary, continue your notes on the back of this page, on note cards, or in a word-processing document.

Greek Hero or Heroine: _____

Main Idea _____
_____
_____

Quotation or Paraphrase _____
_____
_____
_____
_____

Source Information _____
_____
_____
_____
_____

Main Idea _____
_____
_____

Quotation or Paraphrase _____
_____
_____
_____
_____

Source Information _____
_____
_____
_____
_____

Main Idea _____
_____
_____

Quotation or Paraphrase _____
_____
_____
_____
_____

Source Information _____
_____
_____
_____
_____

Main Idea _____
_____
_____

Quotation or Paraphrase _____
_____
_____
_____
_____

Source Information _____
_____
_____
_____
_____

All-in-One Workbook
© Pearson Education, Inc. All rights reserved.

Name _____ Date _____

"Perseus," by Edith Hamilton
Take Notes for Writing to Sources

Planning Your Argument: Before you begin drafting your **response to literature**, use the chart below to organize your ideas. Follow the directions at the top of each box.

1. Write a thesis statement that clearly presents your position.
_____
_____
_____
_____
_____

2. Write details that suggest Perseus was a true hero.	**3.** Write details that suggest Perseus was NOT a true hero.

4. Write your conclusion. Summarize your main points and end with a strongly worded restatement of your thesis.
_____
_____
_____
_____
_____

All-in-One Workbook
© Pearson Education, Inc. All rights reserved.

Name _____ Date _____

"The Washwoman" by Isaac Bashevis Singer
Vocabulary Builder

Selection Vocabulary

atonement   pious   rancor

A. DIRECTIONS: *Revise each sentence so that the italicized vocabulary word is used logically. Be sure not to change the vocabulary word.*

1. Her voice was filled with *rancor* as she thanked her guests for the wonderful gifts.
   _____

2. He sought *atonement* from the man whom he had rescued.
   _____

3. Because she was *pious*, she ignored the traditions of the Sabbath.
   _____

Academic Vocabulary

align   emigration   exemplify

B. DIRECTIONS: *Write the letter of the word or phrase that is the best synonym for the italicized word. Then use the italicized word in a complete sentence.*

_____ 1. *exemplify*

    A. to be an example of   C. to become aware of

    B. to wish for   D. to show excellence

_____

_____ 2. *align*

    A. to disparage   C. to line up with

    B. to endanger or harm   D. to misunderstand

_____

_____ 3. *emigration*

    A. forgetfulness   C. movement from a region

    B. treason   D. blessing or praise

_____

Name _____ Date _____

"The Washwoman," by Isaac Bashevis Singer
Take Notes for Discussion

Before the Partner Discussion: Read the following passage from the selection. Then, fill out the chart below with ideas you would like to discuss and examples from the text that support your ideas.

> A donkey may permit himself to fall under his burden, but not a human being, the crown of creation.

Discussion Questions	My Ideas	Examples from the Text
1. What does the contrast between the beast of burden and "the crown of creation" suggest about the washwoman?		
2. Does the washwoman's effort make her heroic or merely human? Explain.		

During the Discussion: As you discuss each question, take notes on how your partner's ideas either differ from or build upon your own.

Discussion Questions	Other Ideas Expressed	Comparison to My Own Ideas
1. What does the contrast between the beast of burden and "the crown of creation" suggest about the washwoman?		
2. Does the washwoman's effort make her heroic or merely human? Explain.		

Name _____ Date _____

"The Washwoman" by Isaac Bashevis Singer
Take Notes for Research

As you research the **emigration of Jews from Poland in the years leading up to World War II,** you can use the forms below. First, indicate whether the source is a primary or secondary source. As necessary, continue your notes on the back of this page, on note cards, or in a word-processing document.

Source Information   Check one: ☐ Primary Source   ☐ Secondary Source

Title: _____   Author: _____

Publication Information: _____

Page(s): _____

Main Idea: _____

_____

Quotation or Paraphrase: _____

_____

Source Information   Check one: ☐ Primary Source   ☐ Secondary Source

Title: _____   Author: _____

Publication Information: _____

Page(s): _____

Main Idea: _____

_____

Quotation or Paraphrase: _____

_____

Source Information   Check one: ☐ Primary Source   ☐ Secondary Source

Title: _____   Author: _____

Publication Information: _____

Page(s): _____

Main Idea: _____

_____

Quotation or Paraphrase: _____

All-in-One Workbook
© Pearson Education, Inc. All rights reserved.

Name _____ Date _____

"The Washwoman," by Isaac Bashevis Singer
Take Notes for Writing to Sources

Planning Your Narrative: Before you begin drafting your **story**, use the chart below to organize your ideas. Follow the directions at the top of each box.

1. Jot down notes about Singer's description of the washwoman. Make sure that you keep these characteristics in mind as you draft your story.
_____
_____
_____
_____
_____

2. Create a conflict that shapes the washwoman's earlier years. What obstacle or problem might she have had to overcome? Write notes to help you craft your plot.
_____
_____
_____
_____
_____

3. Add dialogue and details to make your plot interesting and realistic.
_____
_____
_____
_____
_____

4. Write a conclusion that tells how the washwoman solved the conflict. Make your conclusion suggest a progression into Singer's story, something that happens in the washwoman's future.
_____
_____
_____
_____
_____

Name _____ Date _____

from **The Hero's Adventure** by Joseph Campbell and Bill Moyers
Vocabulary Builder

Selection Vocabulary

elixir   motif   psyche

A. Directions: *Provide an explanation for your answer to each question.*

1. What type of *elixir* might appear in a science fiction story, and what would the elixir do?

   _____
   _____

2. How would you describe the *psyche* of an explorer at the moment that he or she makes a discovery?

   _____
   _____

3. What is the usual *motif* of a fable?

   _____
   _____

Academic Vocabulary

colloquial   stance

B. Directions: *Complete each sentence with a word, phrase, or clause that contains a context clue for the italicized word.*

1. To let the group know that they were running late, the guide shouted the *colloquial* expression,

   "_____."

2. To summarize her *stance* on the issue, Anshu said, "_____
   _____."

Name _____ Date _____

from *The Hero's Adventure* by Joseph Campbell and Bill Moyers
Take Notes for Discussion

Before the Debate: Read the following passage from the selection. Then, fill out the chart below with ideas you would like to use in the debate and examples from the text that support your points. The discussion questions will provide a good basis for organizing your thoughts.

> Otto Rank makes the point that there is a world of people who think that their heroic act in being born qualifies them for the respect and support of their whole community.

Discussion Questions	My Ideas	Examples from the Text
1. Is the sheer act of being born heroic? Why or why not?		
2. Should a heroic act qualify a person for the respect and support of the whole community?		

During the Debate: As you discuss each question, take notes on how other students' ideas either differ from or build upon your own.

Discussion Questions	Other Ideas Expressed	Comparison to My Own Ideas
1. Is the sheer act of being born heroic? Why or why not?		
2. Should a heroic act qualify a person for the respect and support of the whole community?		

All-in-One Workbook

Name _____ Date _____

from **The Hero's Adventure** by Joseph Campbell and Bill Moyers
Take Notes for Research

As you research the **"origin story"** about a hero in a narrative work, you can use the organizer below to take notes from your sources. First, identify the character and the work in which he or she appears. Then, take notes, continuing if necessary on note cards or in a word-processing document.

Name of Hero: _____ **Work:** _____

Main Idea _____

Quotation or Paraphrase _____

Source Information _____

Main Idea _____

Quotation or Paraphrase _____

Source Information _____

Main Idea _____

Quotation or Paraphrase _____

Source Information _____

Main Idea _____

Quotation or Paraphrase _____

Source Information _____

Name _____ Date _____

from The Hero's Adventure by Joseph Campbell and Bill Moyers
Take Notes for Writing to Sources

Planning Your Argument: Before you begin drafting your **persuasive essay,** use the chart below to organize your ideas.

1. Take notes about Campbell's definition of the heroic journey.

_____
_____
_____
_____
_____
_____
_____

2. Take a stance.

(Circle one)   Motherhood does fit the pattern.   Motherhood does not fit the pattern.

Take notes to support your point with facts and reasons.

_____
_____
_____
_____
_____
_____
_____
_____

3. Draft a thesis statement to clearly state your position in the introduction of your essay.

_____
_____
_____
_____
_____
_____
_____

All-in-One Workbook
© Pearson Education, Inc. All rights reserved.

Name _____ Date _____

from My Hero: Extraordinary People on the Heroes Who Inspire Them by Elie Wiesel
Vocabulary Builder

Selection Vocabulary

    embody   recalcitrant   surmount

A. DIRECTIONS: *Complete each sentence with a word, phrase, or clause that contains a context clue for the italicized word.*

1. To *embody* the characteristics of a hero, a person would _____
_____

2. To succeed, a hero needs to *surmount* _____
_____

3. A *recalcitrant* child needs _____
_____

Academic Vocabulary

    ambiguity   ultimately   underscore

B. DIRECTIONS: *Think about the meaning of each italicized word. Then answer each question with a complete sentence.*

1. Do most stubborn people *ultimately* learn to cooperate and accept the ideas of others?
_____

2. What would you do to *underscore* the depth of your feelings when talking to a friend?
_____

3. What sometimes causes *ambiguity* in the answers to open-ended questions?
_____

Name _____ Date _____

from **My Hero: Extraordinary People on the Heroes Who Inspire Them** by Elie Wiesel
Take Notes for Discussion

Before the Group Discussion: Read the following passage from the selection.

> Is a hero a hero twenty-four hours a day, no matter what? Is he a hero when he orders his breakfast from a waiter? Is he a hero when he eats it? What about a person who is not a hero, but who has a heroic moment?

During the Discussion: As you discuss each question, take notes on how other students' ideas either differ from or build upon your own.

Discussion Questions	Other Ideas Expressed	Comparison to My Own Ideas
1. Why does Wiesel ask these questions?		
2. How do you answer each of these questions? How might Wiesel answer these questions?		
3. How do these questions clarify the problem Wiesel sees in defining *heroism*?		

Name _____ Date _____

from My Hero: Extraordinary People on the Heroes Who Inspire Them by Elie Wiesel
Take Notes for Research

As you research **one of the false heroes that Wiesel mentions,** you can use the organizer below to take notes from your sources. At the top, identify the false hero that you have chosen for your topic. Then use the form to collect your information. As necessary, continue your notes on the back of this page, on note cards, or in a word-processing document.

False Hero: _____.

Main Idea _____
_____

Quotation or Paraphrase _____
_____
_____
_____
_____

Source Information _____
_____
_____
_____
_____

Main Idea _____
_____

Quotation or Paraphrase _____
_____
_____
_____
_____

Source Information _____
_____
_____
_____
_____

Main Idea _____
_____

Quotation or Paraphrase _____
_____
_____
_____
_____

Source Information _____
_____
_____
_____
_____

Main Idea _____
_____

Quotation or Paraphrase _____
_____
_____
_____
_____

Source Information _____
_____
_____
_____
_____

All-in-One Workbook
© Pearson Education, Inc. All rights reserved.

Name _____ Date _____

from **My Hero: Extraordinary People on the Heroes Who Inspire Them** by Elie Wiesel
Take Notes for Writing to Sources

Planning Your Argument: Before you begin drafting your **definition essay,** use the chart below to organize your ideas. Follow the directions at the top of each section.

1. Summarize Wiesel's definitions:

hero: _____
_____

heroism: _____
_____

2. Summarize your definitions, based on reading and personal experiences:

hero: _____
_____

heroism: _____
_____

3. Note evidence to support your position:

(1) from Wiesel's essay:
_____
_____
_____
_____

(2) from your own readings and experiences:
_____
_____
_____
_____

Name _____ Date _____

"Of Altruism, Heroism and Nature's Gifts in the Face of Terror," by Natalie Angier
Vocabulary Builder

Selection Vocabulary

    accrued   altruism   indomitable

A. DIRECTIONS: *Decide whether each statement below is true or false. On the line before each item, write* **TRUE** *or* **FALSE.** *Then explain your answers.*

_____ 1. Greedy people are often guilty of <u>altruism</u>.

_____ 2. The people who survived the shipwreck of *Titanic* seemed to have been <u>indomitable</u>.

_____ 3. People are generally pleased when they see that their savings have <u>accrued</u> interest.

Academic Vocabulary

    comprise   establish   prevalent

B. DIRECTIONS: *Follow each direction.*

1. Write a sentence about the states that make up the United States. Use the word *comprise*.

2. Write a sentence about a company or an organization you would like to start sometime in the future. Use the word *establish*.

3. Write a sentence about a garden or a forest. Use the word *prevalent*.

Name _____ Date _____

"Of Altruism, Heroism and Nature's Gifts in the Face of Terror," by Natalie Angier
Take Notes for Discussion

Before the Write and Share Session: Read the following passage from the selection. Then, fill out the chart below with ideas you would like to discuss and examples from the text that support your ideas.

> "For every 50 people making bomb threats now to mosques," he said, "there are 500,000 people around the world behaving just the way we hoped they would, with empathy and expressions of grief. We are amazingly civilized."
>
> True, death-defying acts of heroism may be the province of the few. For the rest of us, simple humanity will do.

Discussion Questions	My Ideas	Examples from the Text
1. What does Angier mean by "simple humanity"?		
2. Is "simple humanity" enough? Why or why not?		

During the Write and Share Session: As you discuss each question, take notes on how your partner's ideas either differ from or build upon your own.

Discussion Questions	Other Ideas Expressed	Comparison to My Own Ideas
1. What does Angier mean by "simple humanity"?		
2. Is "simple humanity" enough? Why or why not?		

Name _____ Date _____

"Of Altruism, Heroism and Nature's Gifts in the Face of Terror" by Natalie Angier
Take Notes for Research

As you research **the relief efforts that occurred in the aftermath of the events of September 11, 2001,** use the chart below to take notes from your sources. As necessary, continue your notes on the back of this page, on note cards, or in a word-processing document.

Relief Efforts That Occurred Following September 11, 2001	
Main Idea _____ Quotation or Paraphrase _____ Source Information _____ 	Main Idea _____ Quotation or Paraphrase _____ Source Information _____
Main Idea _____ Quotation or Paraphrase _____ Source Information _____ 	Main Idea _____ Quotation or Paraphrase _____ Source Information _____

Name _____ Date _____

"Of Altruism, Heroism and Nature's Gifts in the Face of Terror," by Natalie Angier
Take Notes for Writing to Sources

Planning Your Argument: Before you begin drafting your **article or blog post**, use the chart below to organize your ideas. Follow the directions at the top of each box.

---

1. Define *altruism* and *heroism*.

_____
_____
_____
_____
_____

---

2. Write examples of altruism and heroism that Angier mentions.	**3.** Write examples of altruism and heroism that you have observed in your own life.

---

4. Use your notes to write a strong thesis statement. You will use it in the introduction of your article or blog post, and you will restate it in your conclusion.

_____
_____
_____
_____
_____

Name _____ Date _____

American Blood Donation
Vocabulary Builder and Take Notes for Writing to Sources

Academic Vocabulary

    distinct   implicitly   underscores

DIRECTIONS: *Complete each sentence with a word, phrase, or clause that contains a context clue for the underlined word.*

1. The distinct sections of an essay include _____
   _____

2. She implicitly expressed her agreement with the proposal by _____
   _____

3. This textbook underscores important terms by using _____
   _____

Take Notes for Writing to Sources

Planning Your Summary: Before you begin drafting the **summary of your findings,** use the chart below to organize your research.

1. Sources:
_____
_____
_____

2. Information gathered and direct quotations:
_____
_____
_____
_____
_____
_____
_____
_____

3. Conclusion to your summary:
_____
_____
_____